Get Inspired to Retire

Get Inspired to Retire

OVER 150 IDEAS to help find your retirement.

DAVID SAYLOR and
GREG HEFFINGTON
with Susan J. Marks

Dearborn™
Trade Publishing
A **Kaplan Professional** Company

President, Dearborn Publishing: Roy Lipner
Vice President and Publisher: Cynthia A. Zigmund
Acquisitions Editor: Victoria Smith
Design: Pletka Design

© 2006 by David Saylor and Greg Heffington

Published by Dearborn Trade Publishing
A Kaplan Professional Company

Printed in the United States of America

06 07 08   10 9 8 7 6 5 4 3 2 1

Library of Congress Cataloging-in-Publication Data

Saylor, David.
    Get inspired to retire : over 150 ideas to help find your retirement /
    David Saylor and Greg Heffington.
        p.   cm.
    ISBN-13: 978-1-4195-3568-0
    ISBN-10: 1-4195-3568-4
    1. Retirement—United States—Planning. I. Heffington, Greg. II. Title.
    HQ1063.2.U6S393 2006
    646.7'9—dc22

                                                                    2005028894

For Mom and Dad:
I am what I am because you were where you were—
always there when I needed you.

David Saylor

For my wife, Barbara, and my daughters, Nicole
and Ashley. You have endured my travel with grace
and understanding. I owe you so much.

Greg Heffington

Contents

Introduction

Thinking about retirement and drawing a blank? Read on! It could be time for some retirement "goal mining." Beyond the finances of it all, would you like to retire early, keep working, cut back, quit, or even change careers? Are you hoping for great adventures or soul-satisfying serenity? Would you like to go back to school or back to your roots? Would you prefer to fish for peacock bass in Brazil or work with the elderly in your hometown? What about a cross-country bicycle trek or a dip in Iceland's Blue Lagoon?

Americans who are approaching retirement age today—those 76 million baby boomers born between 1946 and 1964 who grew up with Woodstock, the Vietnam War, and rock 'n' roll—have their own ideas about what getting older means. And their ideas are far different from their parents'. As with most every other aspect of life they touch, boomers are transforming retirement too. At age 65, they're not ready to head out to pasture and into retirement homes.

If you really haven't thought much about your retirement beyond the "not get up so early" or "spend more time…" (in the garden, golfing, outdoors, riding, reading, or whatever), you're not alone. Many other Americans have no set plans for retirement either.

That can be a problem. How do you determine how much money you'll need to save for retirement if you don't know what you'll be doing then? The typical numbers that investors give financial planners are wild guesses at best. At worst, you may quickly run out of money and fail to accomplish the goals and dreams you worked so hard to achieve.

That's where *Get Inspired to Retire,* with its unique and holistic approach to retirement needs, can help. This book isn't concerned with the details of your 401(k) retirement plan, if you've invested your savings wisely, or whether you're buying the right investment product. It isn't designed to sell a product or dictate the "right" retirement goals for you either. This isn't about the details of *funding* your retirement.

Get Inspired is about helping you figure out what it is that you would like to do in your future. It recognizes up front that there are many choices available to today's older Americans. Whereas people used to talk about retiring and dying in the same breath, retirement today offers the freedom and opportunity to live your dreams, whatever they may be. The sky and beyond is the limit of what retirees can do in the future.

Age 65 no longer means mandatory retirement, out to pasture, and into a retirement home. Studies show that many Americans actually choose not to retire, whether for financial or other reasons. Seven out of ten older workers (55 and over) continued to work full-time in

2004, according to numbers from the AARP Public Policy Institute. The majority of boomers (eight out of ten) also plan to keep working beyond the conventional retirement age (AARP, *Baby Boomers Envision Retirement II,* 2004).

Get Inspired to Retire will help you see what some of your options are and the role they might play in fulfilling the next adventure in your life. Armed with such insight, you can learn how to make the choices that are right for you.

With its catalog of ideas, pictures, and direction, this book will help you to envision your retirement lifestyle, what you would like to do or not do, where you want to live, and how you would like to spend your vacations, free time, and more. You'll learn ways to fill your day planner—from new work options to old play options—and how to find the housing and style that work for you. This book is full of suggestions for once (or twice) in a lifetime adventures, volunteering options, and legacy alternatives. Some options are over-the-top extravagances; others are on-a-budget reality. This book also offers an array of options to those with health limitations.

We will talk about the importance of balance in life—balance that's necessary for true happiness. It's not enough to play all the time or work incessantly. A fulfilling retirement draws from many areas of life, including work, family, finances, and personal, mental, physical, and spiritual well-being.

This book, we hope, will reawaken your forgotten or dormant dreams, overlooked ideas, and life goals. It will help you design a mission statement for your retirement. You'll begin to understand the role of structure in retirement, and then see how to chart your ideas and goals on a retirement time line—what we call your Retirement Lifeline. Once you know what you want to do and when, you and your financial advisor can realistically determine the amount of money you'll need and plan appropriately to fund the retirement of your choice. Your Lifeline can serve as your guide.

The catalog portion of this book goes beyond just giving you ideas. We'll also provide the following features to help you on your journey:

• **Ultimate:** An experience that's truly memorable.

• **Reality Check:** Important considerations to keep in mind.

• **What It Takes to Get There:** Where you can go for more information.

• **Cost:** A general idea of the expenses involved.

About the Authors

David Saylor is a baby boomer, Certified Senior Advisor, and an expert on investment issues facing boomers and seniors. He's also a vice president of Van Kampen Investments, which is based in Oakbrook Terrace, Illinois, and he focuses on creative development for Van Kampen Consulting. Over the past 20 years, his work experience has ranged from managing a trading desk to retail brokerage, municipal underwriting, and investment marketing. Prior to joining the consulting group, he was responsible for marketing Van Kampen's $25 billion in fixed-income mutual funds.

An adventurer and avid skier, Saylor also is a coauthor with Scott West and Mitch Anthony of *The Financial Professional's StoryBook* (Dearborn Trade Publishing, 2004).

He holds a bachelor's degree in finance with a concentration in investments from Babson College in Wellesley, Massachusetts.

Greg Heffington, also a baby boomer, adventurer, and marathon runner, is a registered corporate coach and has been consulting in the retirement business for almost 20 years. He's a vice president of Van Kampen Investments and a well-known speaker on retirement and investment options. He has shared his mix of humor and energy with more than 50,000 financial professionals, and he's a frequent guest lecturer at the University of Southern California. Heffington's financial services' experience includes working as a retirement plan consultant and owning a retirement-plan administration company.

He holds a bachelor's degree in accounting and taxation from Colorado State University.

A Few Details

Throughout the catalog chapters in Part Two and in the Resources section at the back of the book, we mention various groups and organizations. These are not endorsements of any of these organizations or groups, their programs, or affiliates. They are online destinations that represent a diverse set of ideas and interests where readers may find more information. Also, all prices mentioned are approximate and intended to provide only a general idea of related expenses.

We also use various names in scenarios that illustrate choices and dilemmas faced by real people as they plan for and experience retirement. The names are all fictitious.

Now, get ready to open your mind to today's unlimited world of retirement choices. But remember, you get what you plan for, so plan thoroughly and plan early. Happy dreaming, and happy reality. True freedom is saved for last!

Chapter 1

Welcome to the Age of Choice

Welcome to the age of choice. Whatever your age, how you spend your retirement is up to you. So is where you live, how you spend your time, with whom, when, and how you finance it all.

Imagine your retirement. Perhaps you're lazing on a white, sandy beach set against a brilliant turquoise sea. Or maybe you're at home in your cozy kitchen surrounded by your grandchildren, who are helping you cook dinner. Still another image could be you on your way to an orphanage in the Ukraine where you teach English.

Any and all of these images could contribute to your successful retirement. There is no one right answer or right choice. Retirement in the 21st century is very much a personalized quest that begins with recognizing what it is you truly want out of life. Stop and think about it. What will it take to truly satisfy you in life? That's not an easy question to answer at any age.

A tool that can help is Retirement Imaging, or imagining what you would like to be doing in your retirement or senior years. Then, think about how and what it will take to achieve your dreams. You will find Retirement Imaging exercises in the pages that follow.

First, keep in mind that the activities and pursuits that made you happy at age 40 will not necessarily make you happy at 70. They may, however, provide some clues about what you would like to do with your future.

Consider Wills who retired early to start a volunteer organization to maintain outdoor trails. At age 40, he was too busy with extreme mountain biking and hiking to be concerned with deteriorating trails. He wasn't married at the time either and spent his time solo on his bike, hiking outdoors, or at work. He didn't have much time or passion for anything else.

As Wills aged—which is true for most of us—he became more aware of the need for balance in his life. Work, hiking, and biking weren't enough anymore. Most of us discover that the family, financial, personal, mental, physical, spiritual, and even career aspects of our lives must be more in balance to heighten our fulfillment.

Once Wills recognized his need for greater balance in his life, he looked to his lifelong love affair with the outdoors for the key to what he wanted to do in retirement.

Perhaps the key to what you might want to do in your later years lies in your past, too. Try answering the following questions as a way to help rekindle some of your goals and dreams. There is no right or wrong answer. This is simply a way to help you begin to think about what is significant in your life. You also can ask your spouse or significant other to answer the questions.

Finding Your Future in Your Past

1. **Favorite Subject:** What was your major in school? Have you fulfilled the goals you set at graduation?

2. **Best Job:** What was the best job of your life? What did you like most about it?

3. **Best Year:** What was the best year of your life? Why?

4. **Best Vacation:** What was your favorite vacation? Why?

5. **Best House:** Of all the houses you have lived in, which was your favorite? Why?

6. **Best Use of Money:** What product, service, gift, or investment has given you the greatest satisfaction?

7. **Favorite Activity:** Of the hobbies, sports, and activities that you've participated in, which was your favorite?

8. **Best Award:** Which award or accomplishment has given you the most pride? Why?

9. **Best Gift:** What gift, favor, or act of kindness you received had the most meaning to you?

Finding Your Balance

You may never have paid much attention to spiritual and religious matters in your earlier years. But suddenly, at age 62, you may find yourself drawn to teach Sunday school at a local church. Or, after years of estrangement, you're driven to reconcile with a family member. These kinds of longings and responses aren't that unusual as we age. In fact, they're a natural part of the aging and maturation process.

Louise, 67, had retired several years earlier, was set financially, and doing all the things she had dreamed of doing, but she still wasn't happy. She hadn't spoken with her sister since their mother died almost 25 years ago. The estrangement never had bothered her before, but in the past year it had become like a nagging body ache that wouldn't go away. Finally Louise called her sister. The relief was almost immediate, and the two had a long chat. In fact, Louise agreed to visit her sister the following spring. With that huge burden lifted, Louise finally could freely enjoy her retirement choices.

Louise had thought through all aspects of her retirement except that one. She had a plan, but one piece of the puzzle was missing until she reconciled with her sister. For others, finding happiness and fulfillment in retirement might not be as obvious.

Happiness can be relatively complicated. It's more than feeling good. It encompasses gratification, fulfillment, finding meaning in your life, and more, says David E. Morrison, Jr., M.D., a Chicago-based psychiatrist, recognized executive coach, and consultant to cities and senior management at Fortune 500 companies.

We may find a clue about what makes us happy in retirement from what others say. AARP, the 35-million-member nonprofit organization devoted to advocacy, information, and help to those over 50, annually looks at baby boomers' attitudes and actions. In the 2004 survey, *Boomers at Midlife: The AARP Life Stage Study,* Princeton Survey Research Associates International talked to more than 2,250 boomers, ages 38 to 56, about what aspect of their lives mattered most. Almost four in ten (39 percent) said personal relations with family and friends was the most important; a little less than a quarter (24 percent) pointed to religious or spiritual life, and 19 percent cited physical health as the most important life area.

Most Important Life Area for Boomers

Which one of these areas is most important to you?

Relations with family and friends:	39 percent
Religious or spiritual life:	24 percent
Physical health:	19 percent
Personal finances:	8 percent
Mental health:	4 percent
Work or careers*:	3 percent
Leisure activities:	1 percent

* Asked only of those employed either full- or part-time

Source: *Boomers at Midlife 2004: The AARP Life Stage Study*

Let's take a closer look at what matters to you. How do you divide your time now among:

- **Work** (including your career, consulting, and charity)

- **Family** (including friends and social groups)

- **Self** (including hobbies, self-improvement, and solitude)

How would you like to divide your time when you're 65? Use Figure 1.1 from Morrison Associates, Ltd., life and work coaching experts, as a worksheet to help you. Changing how you allocate your time among work, family, and self isn't all that easy. Each area requires a different set of strengths and competencies. Do you have the relationship skills to spend more time with your family? Do they have the skills as well? Will you be mentally and physically able to devote more time to work? Are you independent enough to devote more time to yourself? Keep in mind, adds Morrison, that spending more time in one area means devoting less time in another.

Figure 1.1   Dividing Your Time

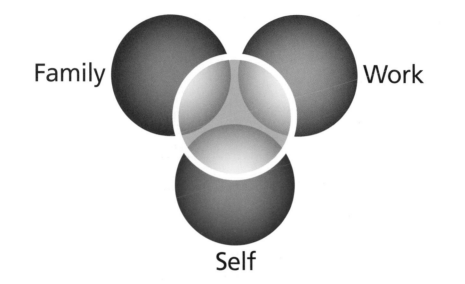

How do you divide your time now between work, self, and family? How would you like to divide your time when you are 65 years old? Changing how you divide your time between work, self, and family is not as easy as it might first appear. Each area requires a different set of strengths and competencies

1. Where are you now? Place a small dot in the white circle representing how you currently divide your time.

2. Where would you like to be at age 65? Place a small square in the white circle representing how you would like to divide your time when your are 65 years old.

3. Optional: ask your spouse to do the same, using a different pen.

Source: Morrison Associates, Ltd.

Let's break down even further what matters to you with the help of a Life Balance Wheel from ACT: Advantage Coaching and Training, life and work specialists. (See Figure 1.2.) The wheel will help you see whether your life is in balance and what areas come up short.

Figure 1.2   Life Balance Wheel

Within each of the following eight areas, circle the number that best represents your level of satisfaction in that area of your life (7 = Completely satisfied; 1 = Completely dissatisfied):

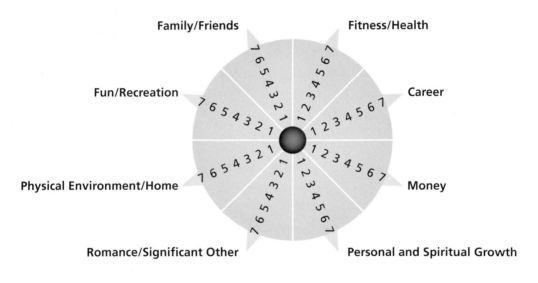

Now connect the dots. The rounder the wheel, the more balanced your life. Imagine how your car would travel if the wheels were in this shape! A coach can aid you to find the balance you desire!

Source: Adapted from *The Confidence Plan* by Tim Ursiny, PhD, CBC, RCC

Is your wheel balanced? If it is and you're happy, that's great. If it's not, that could still be OK. Your happiness relates to your satisfaction, your feelings, and your expectations. In other words, happiness and fulfillment depend on what matters to you—not on someone else's definition or expectations. Keep in mind, too, that a balanced life alone doesn't guarantee happiness, adds Tim Ursiny, PhD, a psychologist, life coach, and author of *The Confidence Plan: How to Build a Stronger You* (Sourcebooks, Inc.).

Try one more exercise to help you further clarify what matters most to you. As we've discussed, for most people aging successfully requires more than money, vacations, health, and relationships. The worksheet in Figure 1.3 will help you gain a sense of control and confidence over your life and your retirement by highlighting your strengths and weaknesses. Remember that meaningful plans and life decisions always involve making choices.

Figure 1.3   Anxiety Scale

For most people, aging successfully requires more than money. It requires satisfaction in the key areas below. For this exercise, place a mark along the scale representing how confident you feel today that you are on track to succeed in each of these areas. Optional: ask your spouse to do the same with a different marker.

Key Area	On Track/Confident	◁ Average ▷	Off Track/High Anxiety
Money			
Career			
Health—Physical			
Health—Mental			
Health—Spiritual			
Relationships—Friends			
Relationship—Spouse			
Relationship—Family			
Relationship—Coworkers			
Home—House			
Home—Location			
Leisure—Hobbies			
Leisure—Vacations			
Leisure—Social			
Self Esteem			

Gaining a sense of control and confidence with regard to retirement can start by addressing the problem areas first. Meaningful plans and big decisions always involve making choices.

What Do You Really Want?

Now that you've thought a bit about what matters to you and where you are today, what is it that you would like to do in your retirement? Again, there is no right or wrong answer. This is all about you and what will satisfy you.

Start by asking yourself the following questions, courtesy of psychologist Ursiny. Have your spouse or partner answer the questions, too.

1. What is it I want in my retirement?

2. Why do I want it? What will achieving it do for me? If I want to play golf, for example, why do I want to play golf?

3. How will I know when I have it?

4. Where do I want to have it? Where do I want to live, for example?

5. With whom do I want to share it?

6. If I get this something, how will it affect other areas of my life? If I want to move to Florida, for example, will that mean I won't see my grandchildren who live in Indiana or Kansas? Will I miss my friends?

7. Beyond money, what resources do I have that can help me get there? If I wish to move, perhaps a family member already lives in the area I'm considering.

8. Again beyond money, what potentially could stop me from achieving what I want to do? My grown children, for example, might not want me to move away.

9. Do I need additional resources to make this happen? If I have a physical disability, for example, will that require added expense or special arrangements?

10. How will I make all this happen? Am I prepared to do it? Do I have the confidence to go ahead and form a plan, and then act on it?

To further help define what it is you want to do in retirement, indicate your preferences on the worksheet in Figure 1.4. This exercise is intended to help you establish direction and vision for retirement and to provide reference points to guide you through the many choices ahead.

Figure 1.4   Preferences

What are your preferences for the years ahead? Place a small mark along each line indicating your preference for each key area. Optional: ask your spouse to do the same with a different marker.

When do you want to retire?

ASAP |————|————|————|————| Never

Will your life be…

The same |————|————|————|————| Very different

Will you live…

Where you are now |————|————|————|————| Far, far away

What will consume your time?

Work |————|————|————|————| Leisure

Will life be…

Calm |————|————|————|————| Busy

Will your days be…

Scheduled |————|————|————|————| Spontaneous

You will prefer to be…

Home |————|————|————|————| Traveling

You will spend time with…

Self |————|————|————|————| Many others

Marking your preferences on each line will help you establish direction and vision for retirement—reference points to help guide you through the many choices to follow.

Your Results

Is a pattern starting to emerge around your potential retirement choices? At the very least, you should begin to recognize what truly matters to you in life. That can be the foundation on which to build your choices. With the pattern or choices in mind, thumb through the catalog portion of this book for ideas on specific things you can do or strive for in your retirement.

Of course, you will encounter roadblocks along the way. You could face either physical, mental, emotional, or fiscal issues. You can minimize some of those issues if you diversify your psychological portfolio. For example, says Morrison, "instead of basing your happiness in retirement on gratification from just one thing, build in plans to use your interests in a number of different things." The retiree who planned her enjoyment in retirement solely around reading was never able to recover her joy in life after she lost her vision. Perhaps if she had developed her love of music or writing, she would have had other possibilities.

Also, beware the temptation to wear yourself out with self-indulgence and dissatisfying frenetic activity. In other words, don't take a trip just so you can say you did or just for something to do if you truly don't want to go. This is the age of choice. Think about your choices, and do what *you* want to do, not what someone says you're supposed to do, says Morrison.

When it comes to the financial issues that threaten your retirement choices, remember that you get what you plan for. Start planning today.

"Instead of basing your happiness in retirement on gratification from just one thing, build in plans to use your interests in a number of different things. This is the age of choice. Think about your choices, and do what you want to do, not what someone says you're supposed to do."

David E. Morrison, MD

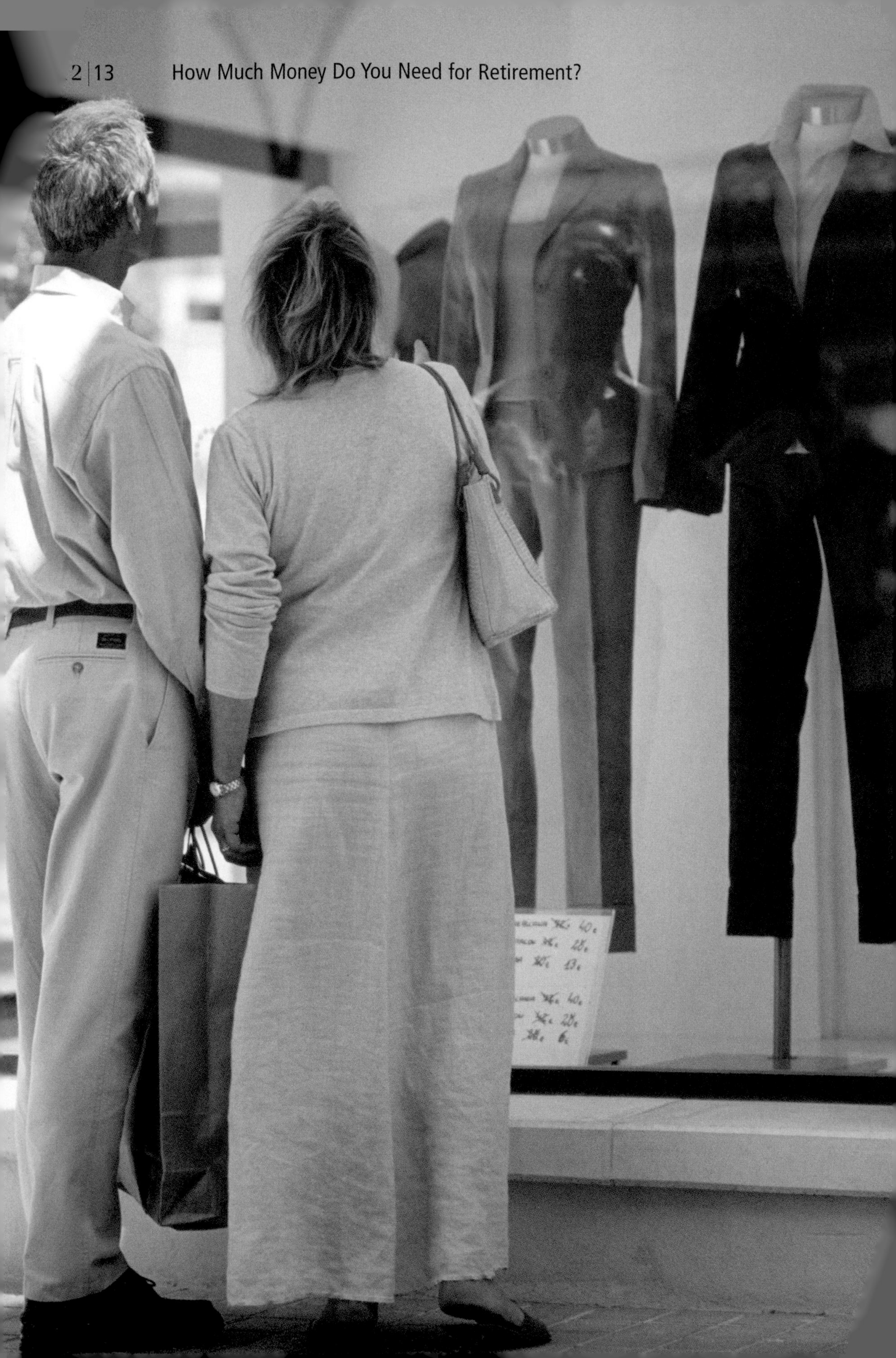

Chapter 2

How Much Money Do You Need for Retirement?

Now that you have an idea of your retirement mentality and an image of the lifestyle you would like to attain, or preserve, in your older years, you're ready to piece it all together. You can do that with the help of a retirement time line, or Lifeline. We'll get into the details of the Lifeline later in this chapter.

First, however, you'll need to take stock of your personal financial situation. The goal of this book is to help you *find* the details of your retirement. The best way to fund those details is up to you and your financial advisor to determine. But it's nonetheless essential to get a realistic overview of your financial situation.

As you do so, remember that your happiness and fulfillment in life are the main objectives. You get what you plan for. Think three steps to success:

• **Chart it** (on your Lifeline, pages 19 – 21).

• **Plan it** (with your advisor).

• **Do it** (your dreams and goals).

How Confident Are You?

Let's approach your financial future in terms of concepts and confidence instead of real numbers.

Figure 2.1   The Money Lines

Retirement is a transition—not a transformation. There's a good chance you won't change much as a consumer. For each of the expenditure categories below, place a mark on your spending habits as compared to others with similar income. Optional: ask your spouse to do the same with a different marker.

	Spend much less than people with similar income.	**Spend the same as people with similar income.**	**Spend much more than people with similar income.**
Home(s)			
Automobiles			
Utilities/Phone			
Credit Card Interest			
Food			
Clothes/Jewelry			
Medical			
Entertainment			
Travel			
Hobbies			
Fitness			
Self-Improvement			
Friends/Family			
Pets			
Charity			

If the average person with similar income needs "x" per month for retirement, you might need:

Retirement

Have you thought much about your spending habits in retirement? Will they change? No matter what you claim or estimate you will spend, there's a good chance your spending habits will remain fairly constant. Retirement is a transition, not a transformation.

Once again, let's look at what others say about their personal finances. Almost one-fourth of the baby boomers (23 percent) participating in the *Boomers at Midlife: The AARP Life Stage Study* point to their finances as the biggest challenge in their lives right now.

More numbers from the *Boomers at Midlife* survey include:

• Only 22 percent of working boomers say they're very satisfied with their personal finances.

• 30 percent haven't met their financial expectations.

• 36 percent say personal finance is the one life area they would like to change most.

• Only 58 percent think they're likely to meet their financial expectations.

Now it's your turn. What do you think about your personal finances? Try the exercise in Figure 2.1.

How confident are you of the ability of your personal finances to meet your needs now and in retirement? Use the Confidence Scale in Figure 2.2 to help you. Zero represents no confidence, you're doomed, and 10 means you have the perfect retirement plan and complete confidence in your personal finances. Rate your current finances first, and then rate your retirement finances. Ask your spouse or partner to try the same exercise.

Figure 2.2   The Confidence Scale

Place a small mark along the line.

0	5	10
No Confidence		Complete Confidence

Next, let's take aim at what specific aspects of your personal finances concern you the most. Check out the Financial Target in Figure 2.3. This chart lets you rate your confidence on a scale of 0 (no confidence) to 7 (totally confident). Be honest with yourself. This is all about helping you make the right choices.

Figure 2.3   **The Financial Target**

How do you feel about your financial situation now? If 7 is completely confident and 0 is no confidence at all, circle one number in each of the ten slices. Then, you'll know where to begin asking questions about your retirement plan. Optional: ask your spouse or partner to do the same with a different marker.

Are you satisfied or shocked by your assessments of your personal financial future? When you really sit down and think about your financial future, you may be in for a rude awakening. But keep in mind that the areas of least confidence represent a starting point for you to ask the right questions of your financial advisor so that you can shore up that area of your retirement plan. Again, you get what you plan for. If you plan ahead based on realistic projections and expectations, you will minimize your chances of running out of money in your lifetime.

Your Retirement Lifeline

Now you're ready to build your Retirement Lifeline—your retirement time line and a mission statement of sorts. (See Figure 2.4.) This is where your dreams, goals, plans, income or entitlements, options, employer pensions, and expenses are all down in writing in one place and on one sheet of paper. It's designed to give you the big picture of your potential retirement.

The Lifeline can include the age at which you will decide to quit work, apply for Social Security, receive Medicare, begin Medigap insurance, pay off your mortgage (if that's your choice), and opt to begin drawing down a pension, 401(k), or other retirement vehicle. The Lifeline also takes into account your life expectancy and, of course, your goals, dreams, and accomplishments.

Don't be afraid of what your Lifeline may reveal. It is a valuable financial planning tool that becomes the basis on which you and your financial advisor, accountant, or lawyer can plan your real-life financial future. If you're honest about assessing your wants, needs, and desires in your older years—as we've discussed already—your Lifeline will be a true reflection of *your* image of retirement. And once you know what it is you would like to do in retirement, you can chart your financial goals and how to achieve them.

Keep in mind that your Lifeline is dynamic and can change. If your wants, needs, or lifestyle change, so can and should your Lifeline change, but don't lose sight of your original goals and needs.

Even if you have only a few ideas for your Lifeline beyond your entitlements, that's OK. It's still a reflection of you and your choices at this moment. The Lifeline is a solid and realistic basis for your financial plan. Take it to your financial planner, lawyer, and/or accountant to help you plan for the future. You might be surprised by how much easier it is for them to help you with beneficial financial, legal, and tax strategies when you know what it is you truly want.

Figure 2.4   Your Retirement Lifeline

Step 1.   Begin by filling in the years corresponding with your ages at the bottom of the Lifeline.

Step 2.   Chart known or contemplated goals on the time line with a pencil (they'll change, so use something erasable) along with the estimated annual income or expense, if any. **Need ideas?** Turn to pages 22 to 139 for the book's catalog of retirement ideas.

Step 3.   Chart the following important dates to the best of your ability.

When will…

☐ Your last mortgage payment—leaves money for other things.

☐ Your children graduate from college—leaves time and money for other things.

☐ Your daughter's 27th birthday and your son's 29th birthday—average marriage age.

☐ Your daughter's 29th birthday and your son's 31st birthday—average age for first-time parents, making you a first-time grandparent.

☐ Age you'd like to retire or phase in retirement—consider the consequences of leaving your employee-sponsored medical, dental, long-term care, and life insurance plans.

☐ Age you would like to start a new career, endeavor, or part-time job.

☐ Age you are entitled to begin withdrawing from your employer-sponsored retirement plan; your plan will specify the age—each is different.

☐ Age you would like to begin distributions from your IRA, Keogh, or other tax-advantaged plan.

☐ Age you would like to apply for Social Security benefits.

Step 4.   Ask your spouse to complete steps 1 through 3, and consolidate your Lifelines.

Remember, this is your retirement and your future.

• **Chart it** (on your Lifeline).

• **Plan it** (with your advisor).

• **Do it** (your dreams and goals).

Mile Markers, Entitlements, and Significant Dates

A Age: **50**

Consider long-term care insurance and annuities, make sure your will is current, and consider drafting a living will.

B Age: **55**

Option to begin 401(k), Keogh, SEP-IRA, and profit-sharing plan distributions if unemployed. May be eligible for pension benefits, depending on the plan and years of service.

C Age: **59 1/2**

Option to begin 401(k), IRA, Keogh, SEP distributions.

Chart It.

Use this space to chart Steps 1, 2, 3, and 4.

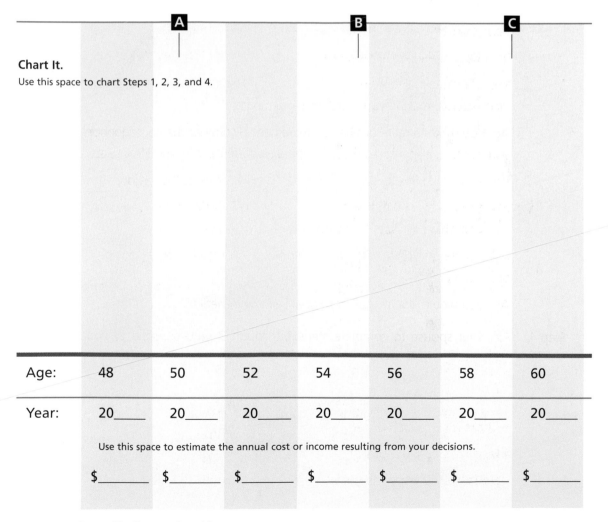

Age:	48	50	52	54	56	58	60
Year:	20____	20____	20____	20____	20____	20____	20____

Use this space to estimate the annual cost or income resulting from your decisions.

$_____ $_____ $_____ $_____ $_____ $_____ $_____

Source: Van Kampen Consulting

Mile Markers, Entitlements, and Significant Dates (continued)

D   Age: **62**

Early Social Security benefits are available (subject to income caps),
but lifetime distributions will be penalized.

E   Age: **65**

Option to apply for Medicare benefits and full Social Security, if born
before 1943. If you postpone Social Security, you'll receive higher benefits.[1]

F   Age: **66**

Option for full Social Security benefits if born before 1960.[1]

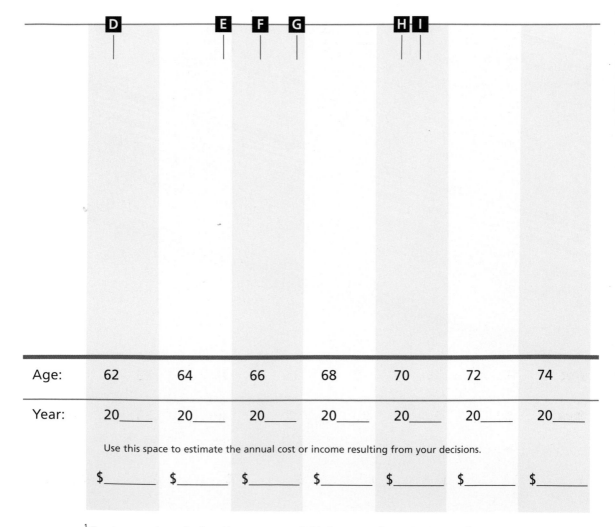

Age:	62	64	66	68	70	72	74
Year:	20____	20____	20____	20____	20____	20____	20____

Use this space to estimate the annual cost or income resulting from your decisions.

| $_____ | $_____ | $_____ | $_____ | $_____ | $_____ | $_____ |

[1] Exact year and month of entitlements are available from your financial advisor or from www.ssa.gov

Age: **67**

Option for full Social Security if born in 1960 or later.

 Age: **70**

Incentive to postpone Social Security ends—begin collecting.

I Age: **70 1/2**

Must begin distributions from traditional IRAs, Keogh, SEP-IRA.

J Age: **81**

Life expectancy for men.[2]

K Age: **84**

Life expectancy for women.[2]

Age:	76	78	80	82	84	86	88
Year:	20____	20____	20____	20____	20____	20____	20____

Use this space to estimate the annual cost or income resulting from your decisions.

$_____ $_____ $_____ $_____ $_____ $_____ $_____

[2] Natural Center for Health Statistics

9 to 5:
Ideas to Fill Your
Day Planner

The choices and the freedom are yours. Whether you opt to make money, make friends, or make macramé, there are plenty of ways to spend your time.

Work

1 Don't Retire
65 Is Not the Finish Line

Reaching age 65 isn't the same milestone it used to be. For most people living in the 21st century, it's simply another year older. Why shouldn't it be just another year for you?

If you enjoy your work, it may make sense to keep going. No one says you must retire. If you're as productive as younger workers and not ready to retire, don't.

Another tidbit: The workplace needs you. A shortage of workers is expected by 2010, as baby boomers begin to retire. How's that for a reason to keep working? The extra income and often health insurance might be nice, if not essential.

Older people have options today that they didn't have 20 or 30 years ago. Sure, 65 in general is the age at which you're eligible to receive Social Security benefits, but you don't have to collect

those benefits just yet. Years ago when Social Security was first available, folks generally lived only a few years beyond age 65 so it was the norm to retire and enjoy those final years. Today, your twilight years may last considerably longer. The senior life expectancy for men is about 81, and for women, about 84.

Don't fret about age discrimination in the workplace, either. Laws have been enacted to protect you from any age bias.

Reality Check:
If you need the extra money, great. If not, put it in trust for the grandkids, donate it to a favorite cause, or spend it on something you've always wanted.

What It Takes to Get There:
www.experienceworks.org; www.go60.com; www.2young2retire.com; from the federal government, www.firstgov.gov, then click on Jobs, Education and Volunteerism; www.aarp.org.

2 Change Careers
Get That Job You've Always Wanted

How many people start their careers by taking a temporary position just until the right job comes along? The trouble is that many of those people wake up 35 years later staring at retirement and still working in a field they never really chose for themselves. That "perfect job" never materialized.

Here's your second chance. Instead of looking at 65 as the end, view it as the beginning. Make that career change. Start over. It's not as scary as you might think. This time around you're armed with

Left and above: Approach 65 as a new beginning in your work life. This is the chance to live your career dreams. Check job sites and job fairs to find the perfect job for you.

the wisdom of age and experience. In fact, if you plan right financially for your older years, starting anew actually frees you. No more regrets. No more what-ifs strewn along the career path.

Plenty of industry, business, and government organizations are available to help you with guidance, training, and education. Don't be intimidated by today's youth-oriented Information Age, either. The workplace needs what you have to offer. So turn on your computer and get cracking. The dream job awaits.

Reality Check:
Workplace discrimination, including that based on age, is prohibited by law.

What It Takes to Get There:
www.experienceworks.org; www.seniorjobbank.com; www.seniors4hire.org; www.careerjournal.com; www.monster.com.

3 Start Your Own Business
Become a Small-Business Owner

Small-business ownership takes vision, business acumen, intense commitment, self-motivation, thorough planning, hard work, and an under-

standing of what it takes to succeed. A great idea and a willingness to work aren't enough. Although you needn't be an expert in business planning or payroll, you do have to recognize your weaknesses and look to outside experts to compensate for them.

Building a small business can be intensely rewarding and satisfying, especially for entrepreneurial spirits. People interested in a quiet retirement may want to think twice about this type of adventure.

Owning your own business sounds like such a great option—freedom to do as you please, when you please; no bosses hovering over your shoulder; your own hours; and no corporate quotas or rules and regulations. It almost sounds too good to be true. Actually, it is!

Owning a small business is like having another child. It dominates your life, your heart, and your soul. If you didn't like 9 to 5, five days a week, at a corporate job, you may not like the 8 to 7:30 six or seven days a week, at your own business. It's worth noting, however, that you might like the longer hours much better when the business—and the potential rewards—are your own.

Reality Check:
Get a thorough, formal business plan before you start. A wealth of resources, online and off, is available to help you.

What It Takes to Get There:
A few of the many helpful sites:
National Federation of Independent Business, www.nfib.org; U.S. Small Business Administration, www.sba.gov; www.business.gov; SCORE, www.score.org; www.entrepreneur.com; www.inc.com.

Be a Part-Timer

Work Less

Phase In Retirement

No one says you have to pull the plug on your career at age 65. Why not opt for less stress and ease into retirement?

Here are some options:

- Consider keeping the job you have but work part-time. Employers often are amenable to such an arrangement, especially if working part-time means forgoing certain benefits.

- Work part-time at a favorite haunt like your neighborhood hardware store or chic boutique. Work as little or as often as you like. You might even be able to get health care benefits.

- Change careers in favor of a part-time one: Realtor, tax preparer, or freelance writer are options, and you often choose your own hours.

Think outside the box. If you're a music aficionado, what about a job as a piano tuner? Horse lovers might like to work as farriers. A retired educator could tutor in a favorite subject.

The options and opportunities are endless because with age, you most likely have the knowledge, expertise, and dependability that employers need and want. You have plenty to offer, and employers know it.

Reality Check:

With pensions and health care no longer a guarantee for many Americans, the savvy approach may be to plan for phased-in retirement. This also could be your chance to start developing the second career you've dreamed of.

What It Takes to Get There:

National Association of Realtors, www.realtor.org; Senior Job Bank for over-50 job seekers, www.seniorjobbank.org; www.clubmedjobs.com; National Tutoring Association, www.ntatutor.org.

Left: Tired of working for someone else? Then don't. Do your homework and start a small business.
Above: Or consider working fewer hours at something you particularly enjoy.

5 Become a Free Agent
Consider Consulting

Whether you're an executive or office assistant, doctor or sales clerk, accountant or cashier, chances are that someone can benefit from and will pay for your expertise.

Name your price and your terms and share your wisdom—virtually with the help of PCs and the Internet or in person. Consulting offers the best of both worlds with supplemental income and plenty of freedom to enjoy the rest of your life. It's also a great way to keep your mind active.

Think creatively when it comes to packaging your services. A cashier with 30 years' experience, for example, could provide training or oversight for any number of companies. A retired chief information officer could work with businesses on purchasing or installing new technology. A retail sales clerk could become a personal shopper.

Of course, a prerequisite to successful consulting is to stay abreast of the newest developments in your line of work. And don't forget to network, network, network.

Reality Check:
Don't be discouraged if you hang out your shingle and twiddle your thumbs for a while. That's typical. It takes time to develop a client base. Try lining up some clients before you retire.

What It Takes to Get There:

www.score.org; www.businessknow-how.com; www.msvas.com from Staffcentrix, virtual assisting experts.

6 Instruct Others
Share Your Knowledge through Teaching

Welcome to the world of teaching. In the classroom, as a tutor, or as a volunteer, older individuals have many opportunities to work with and educate the young and the old.

courses—so do some private schools, continuing education organizations, preschools, and even private groups.

Often, no prior teaching experience is required. Enthusiasm and a willingness to help others are mandatory, however.

Reality Check:
Some jobs require specific degrees, credentials, certificates, or prior experience. Don't overlook virtual classroom options.

What It Takes to Get There:

National Tutoring Association, www.ntatutor.org; www.tutornation.com; check with various schools, community colleges, and local organizations; check want ads and local bulletin boards, especially at colleges and universities.

7 Open Your Doors
Turn Your Home into a Bed-and-Breakfast

If you're a traveler who prefers bed-and-breakfasts to hotels or you're simply dreaming up ways to make extra income, retirement could be the perfect time to open your own B&B. You can purchase an existing B&B, buy a quaint house and fashion it into one, or transform your own home into a charming getaway. Making a house into a B&B can lessen the financial burden of a large historic home.

It's not all fun and frolic, however. A bed-and-breakfast is a small business and must be operated as such to avoid creating a money pit. You need a formal business plan that looks at short- and long-range goals as well as an operating plan and budgets.

Teach pottery classes for a local art guild three days a week, then help preschoolers model clay twice a week. Share your photography skills with high school students during the day and adults at the community college in the evening. Tutor a fifth grader in fractions and a tenth grader in trig, or help a second grader with subtraction. Bolster a competitive gymnast's confidence on the parallel bars. Build teamwork on the basketball court. Help an aspiring young golfer fine-tune her putt. Teach a course in comparative literature and one on the Bible.

Community colleges and free universities often rely on working and retired professionals to teach

Left: Capitalize on the wisdom of your experience as a consultant, whether for fun and gratification or profit.
Above: Teaching others is another option loaded with rewards.

Before you jump hook, line, and sinker into what sounds like a romanticist's adventure, talk to other B&B owners to fully understand what the business involves.

Reality Check:

If you own a B&B, you are in the hospitality industry, which means you provide services to others. If your guests come first—as they must—headaches will often follow.

What It Takes to Get There:

Professional Association of Innkeepers International, www.paii.org; http://bandb.about.com; www.business.com, follow the links to hospitality and lodging industry.

8 Patent Pending
Invent a Whatchamacallit

Channel a chunk of your creative energy into inventing that special gadget you've always wanted but never could find or that unique process to improve an everyday chore. Others have done it, why not you?

Consider gadgets like earmuffs, fish scalers, sticky memo pads, the aluminum can, and Velcro. Each was the brainchild of someone with a better idea.

What qualifies for a patent? According to the U.S. Patent and Trademark Office, processes, manufactured articles, machines, composition of matter, and an improvement of any of the above can be protected by a patent. Design and plant patents also protect ornamental design of a manufactured article and asexually reproduced plant varieties. Literary, dramatic, musical, and artistic works cannot be patented but can be protected by copyright.

Top right: Car genius Henry Ford (1863–1947), left, and inventor Thomas Edison (1847–1931) confer.
Above: Bed-and-breakfasts are popular lodging options. Opposite: Betsy Ross sews the first flag with stars and stripes.

You're not an engineer, you say? Plenty of resources are available to help. If you lack the engineering know-how to design your gadget or carry out the research yourself, pay a specialist to draw up the specs. If you can't build your brainchild, hire someone to do it.

So gear up and get going!

Reality Check:
Obtaining a patent is a costly and complicated process. It requires, among other things, a patentability search to determine if your "invention" has been disclosed before. That search generally must be done by an expert before even applying for a patent. That fee as well as the non-refundable filing fee and other fees can mount up.

What It Takes to Get There:

United Inventors Association, www.uiausa.org; http://inventors.about.com; Academy of Applied Science, www.aas-world.org; Patent, Trademark and Copyright Research Foundation, www.ptcforum.org; U.S. Patent and Trademark Office, www.uspto.gov.

Cost: Patent filing fee, about $100 to $150; issue fee, about $650.

9 Run for Office
Get Things Done Right

Tired of the way things are run in your community, county, state, or beyond? Consider running for political office or getting involved and show others how to do things right.

Start off small. Run for county or district commissioner, town council, or other local positions. They generally pay only a small stipend but build your confidence and political base. Or go for the glory and put your hat in the ring for mayor, state senator, governor, or even national office. Plenty of men and women have translated their business acumen into a successful second career in politics. Former stay-at-home spouses have done it, too.

Politics requires a passion to succeed and the willingness to work hard and sacrifice—a commitment your family must make as well.

Rally your troops—that is, volunteers—collect those signatures, and get to work. Don't expect the campaign road to be easy. It rarely is.

Small communities especially offer opportunities and the chance to effect real change.

Reality Check:
This is not a go-it-alone option. Before deciding to run for an office, thoroughly discuss the ramifications with a spouse, loved ones, and friends.

What It Takes to Get There:

www.politicalgrassroots.org; Grassroots Enterprise, www.grassroots.com; www.vote-smart.org; Women in Government Relations, www.wgr.org; www.e-thepeople.org.

BETSY ROSS MAKING THE FIRST FLAG WITH STARS AND STRIPES.

10 Profit from a Passion
Turn a Hobby into a Career

Chances are you've acquired considerable skills and knowledge over the years you've spent enjoying a hobby, arts and crafts, or collectibles. Maybe you've spent your spare time refinishing furniture, making quilts, or collecting pewter. Why not turn your expertise or collection into extra income? Craft fairs are eager for vendors, and local want ads and eBay or other online auction sites provide access to a huge marketplace, whether you want to sell off pieces of Lalique, your hand-knit Christmas stockings, or garage-sale castoffs you've transformed.

Set up your own shop, or at least have that option. You also can devote your efforts to family, friends, and charities. Whatever your choice, be honest with yourself about the quality of your work. Also keep in mind that if you like what you do, someone else will, too.

You could also donate your products to local charities and benefit auctions as a way to help others and generate interest in your handiwork or product.

Reality Check:

If you do go commercial with your talents, approach the work like a business. That's sometimes tough when it involves something you truly enjoy doing, but it's essential for your peace of mind and the success of your business.

What It Takes to Get There:

http://collectibles.about.com; www.acguide.com; www.craftsfaironline.com; www.geezer.com; www.goantiques.com; www.ebay.com or other auction sites.

11 Entertain an Old Idea
Trade on Your Talent

Have you long harbored a secret dream of being a singer, comedian, dancer, or actor? Do others consider you entertaining? "Play the piano for us, Mary!" "Dave, you're a real comedian!" "Marty, show us that dance routine one more time!"

Retirement is the perfect time to give your dream a shot. Community and dinner theaters always need volunteers, whether it's for a puppet show, musical, play, or even cabaret. If you have talent, it won't be long before you move from backstage to upstage. Church and community choirs and bands audition often, and many "comedy stores" hold open-mike nights where the Average Joe can find out just how funny he is.

What have you got to lose? Trade on your skills and have a blast doing it.

Reality Check:
Be realistic and honest with yourself about your skill level. You may need to take some lessons or classes before you're ready for the spotlight.

What It Takes to Get There:
The WWW Virtual Library Theatre and Drama, www.vl-theatre.com; www.voiceofdance.com; www.theatrebooks.com.

12 Where Dreams Come True
Create Your Own Studio

Now that the kids are gone, why not turn that extra bedroom into a studio where you can play with your oil paints, woodworking, ceramics, scrapbooking, sewing, quilting, or other crafts?

If you don't have a spare room, you can screen off part of the family room, dining room, or garage—even part of a large laundry room can be a cozy spot for a studio nook or sewing room. And if you're fortunate enough to own a property with a barn or other outbuildings, you have no excuse not to create a space to create!

A detached garage works great, too. Remodel it into a studio and add a loft so it can double as a guesthouse. Be sure to spring for the additional cost of plumbing. It will make the workspace much more inviting and facilitate cleanup.

Reality Check:
Certain hobbies, such as oil painting or woodworking, can involve fumes or dust. Be sure your studio has proper ventilation.

What It Takes to Get There:
www.craftsreport.com; www.bobvila.com; www.hgtv.com; www.artsuppliesonline.com.

Cost: Your time and whatever materials are needed for the project.

Far left: Pottery can net cool cash. Left: Your musical talents can prove lucrative, too. Above right: You'll enjoy your artistic passions more if you create a special place to pursue them.

13 On the Road Again
Drive a School Bus or Shuttle

If you like kids and like to drive, why not get paid to perform a public service? Driving a school bus can keep you connected with the younger generation while still giving you plenty of time to spend the day your way. You'll most likely get summers off, too.

Local school districts often provide paid driver training, and some even offer benefits.

If you're not up to the task of hauling kids, consider transporting seniors for assisted-living centers, nursing homes, and other facilities. You might also consider driving a handicapped-accessible van or shuttle. Places like Disney World or college campuses often need internal bus drivers. And don't overlook regional transportation districts, either. You might also think about driving a mall or shuttle bus.

Reality Check:
For school bus duty, you'll probably need to be an early riser and not easily distracted. A busload of kids is a big responsibility. These days you'll need to be able to discipline kids if necessary.

What It Takes to Get There:

www.careeroverview.com and click on transportation; www.strategietraining.com; www.schoolbusinfo.org; National Association for Pupil Transportation, www.napt.org.

14 The Write Choice
Pen That Tome, Poem, Prose, or Play

How many people talk about writing the great American novel but never put pen to paper (or fingers to keyboard)? Now is your opportunity to put those great ideas into a manuscript for posterity and, possibly, profit. Perhaps you've daydreamed of writing a historical novel, an episode of a TV sit-com, a collection of poems, a one-act play, or a short story.

Talk to professionals, network, attend writers' workshops, learn the ins and outs of the craft, and then pull up a chair and start writing. Be sure to expect all kinds of detours to finishing

your project, including interruptions (delivery people have no sense of timing) and writer's block (yes, it's real).

If that's not enough to dampen your spirits, you face the daunting prospect of selling your work, if that's your goal.

Still want to write? Some good places to start are The Burry Man Writers Center, a huge umbrella Web site with a lode of information on all forms of writing that covers everything from structure to finding an agent. Two other good resources are Sun Oasis Jobs and JournalismJobs.com.

Reality Check:
Don't be discouraged by rejection or criticism. It's all part of the process of becoming a better writer.

What It Takes to Get There:
The Burry Man Writers Center,
www.burryman.com; www.writing-world.com;
www.writersretreatworkshop.com;
www.placesforwriters.com; www.sunoasis.com;
www.journalismjobs.com.

15 Shopping Sleuth
Become a Mystery Shopper

This is serious—and big—business. After all, in today's competitive retail environment, customer service and satisfaction often make the difference in a sale. Mystery shoppers evaluate not only customer service but store operations, employee integrity, merchandising, product quality, and more.

Usually after a shopping experience that could last less than an hour, the mystery shopper completes a specific questionnaire or other related document.

This can be a great part-time job, but it can take time to establish your reputation and reliability, and to build up a clientele.

Reality Check:
For those who love to shop, does it get any better than getting paid to shop? Be leery of any organization, individual, or company that asks you to pay to become a mystery shopper, warns the Mystery Shopping Providers Association of North America.

What It Takes To Get There:
Mystery Shopping Providers Association,
www.mysteryshop.org; www.markettrends.com,
then click on Mystery Shopper; www.shopnchek.com;
www.serviceintelligence.com.

Cost: Companies pay you to shop and evaluate.

Top left: Driving a school bus offers unique challenges. Left: William Shakespeare overcame odds to become a writer. You can, too. Above: Imagine getting paid to shop. That's the ticket for a mystery shopper.

Volunteer

16 The Gift of Time

Work as a Counselor, Social Worker, Aide, and More

If you have a sympathetic nature and enjoy helping people, consider using your skills to provide crisis counseling, legal advice, or even companionship for the homebound, low-income, and more. Community organizations often provide these kinds of services at no or low cost.

Youth-oriented community organizations welcome older volunteers who have unique wisdom and patience, too.

In searching for the right fit for your talents, you might check out the USA Freedom Corps, Senior Medicare Patrol, SCORE, Points of Light Foundation and Volunteer Center National Network, EASI (Environmental Alliance for Senior Involvement), and Civic Ventures. Each has its own unique approach to helping others.

Reality Check:

The work is gratifying, although some situations may be emotionally draining. Mileage related to the work generally is tax deductible.

What It Takes to Get There:

The federal government's Administration on Aging, www.aoa.gov, click on Elders and Families and follow the many links; www.freedomcorps.gov; www.score.org; www.pointsoflight.org; www.experiencecorps.org; www.easi.org; www.civicventures.org; www.experiencecorps.org.

17 Docents, from Art to Zoo

Cultural Institutions of Every Stripe Need You

Learn why the rhinoceros paces in the zoo, why Georges Seurat painted four views of the harbor at Gravelines, or the reason for T. rex's short forearms.

Volunteering as a docent at a local zoo or art, science, history, or cultural museum can be a fun way for you as well as museum visitors to learn about the unusual and the norm. Most museums provide free or low-cost training for their docents and potential docents that might even include college-level coursework with grades optional.

What a great way to return to school to study a favorite topic and then share your newfound knowledge with others! Hours often are flexible, and the gratitude of others is unmistakable. It's also a great way to meet and develop a circle of friends with interests similar to yours. Some docent programs even organize special trips for fellow docents.

Reality Check:

Being a docent takes a commitment. Museums depend on their volunteers, but for the most part the hours you work are up to you.

What It Takes to Get There:

Contact a local museum; alternatively, American Association for Museum Volunteers, www.acnatsci.org/hosted/aamv; American Association of Museums, www.aam-us.org; Association of Volunteer Administration, www.avaintl.org; National Docent Symposium Council, www.docents.net; Points of Light Foundation and Volunteer Center National Network, www.pointsoflight.org.

18 Peer Joy
Local Senior Centers Welcome Help

Don't hesitate to get involved in a senior group near you. Join the fun, and help others at the same time. It's an intensely rewarding experience and a great way to meet people and make new friends.

Do you like to dance? How about painting or cooking, playing cards, or even reading bestsellers? Are you interested in studying the history and culture of your town, state, and beyond? If so, why not volunteer to lead activities at your local senior center? Those centers can be private, secular, or public, large or small, and generally all welcome volunteers. Religious as well as local ethnic groups also often operate senior centers or programs for older people, and appreciate volunteers. Activities can include private or group lessons, city tours or field trips, regular meetings, and more.

Reality Check:

Senior centers are lifelines for many elderly individuals. They can be a connection for you, too.

What It Takes to Get There:

Check out the center nearest you, or the National & Community Service Senior Corps' Senior Companions, www.seniorcorps.org. Alternatively, check with your church or other religious or ethnic organization.

Top left: Your counsel and advice can make a difference. Top right: There's bingo and lots more at local senior centers. Above: Zoos and aquariums often count on docent volunteers.

19 Find Your Harmony
Join a Choir

For those who love to sing or play music but lament the opportunity to truly do it with verve, think about joining a choir. Religious groups chronically need volunteer choir members, and often you needn't belong to a specific church or denomination. Many communities support musical groups, too—from classical to jazz to a cappella.

It's all about the music and sharing it with others.

If you can't find a group in your area, start your own. Plenty of places—including hospitals, nursing and retirement homes, and community festivals—welcome musicians and singers.

Remember, however, that if you do join a choir, a commitment is required from you.

Reality Check:
If you're single and don't like to go out alone, or don't like to drive at night, chances are a choir director or fellow member gladly will provide transportation. You just have to ask!

What It Takes to Get There:
Check online and in community publications for various organizations in your area; www.elderhostel.org.

Cost: Your time.

20 Skier Safety
Join the National Ski Patrol

Attention all skiers, Nordic and Alpine, boarders, and even nonskiers; the National Ski Patrol (NSP) may need volunteers like you. Though people most often think of the ski patrol as those on-slope hunks and babes who transport the injured, the National Ski Patrol is that and a whole lot more.

In addition to providing on-slope rescue or off-slope emergency care to injured or ill guests, NSP is about education and communication. NSP members get comprehensive outdoor emergency training, too.

Contact ski patrol directors at individual ski areas for more information on qualifications and skills required.

Reality Check:
Major resorts can have qualified retirees as members of their ski patrols. So if you're a skier or boarder who dreams of skiing or riding all day during ski season, apply today. For those outdoor enthusiasts who may not be quite up for the ski patrol, try an outdoor adventure club like The Mountaineers instead.

What It Takes to Get There:
www.nsp.org; check the various resort Web sites and also regional and local ski patrol sites; www.mountaineers.org.

Cost: Training depends on individual resort qualifications requirements.

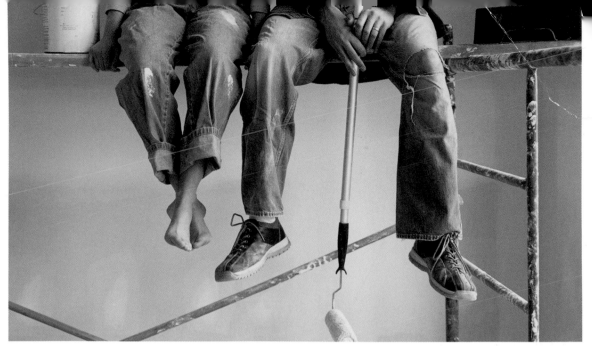

Homework

Home Improvements
Upgrade Your House, Garden, or Property

Your time is just as valuable after retirement as it was before. The big difference, however, is that you have more of it. Take the opportunity to tackle that home addition or do the kitchen remodel you've always talked about but never had time to do. Hire experts or do it yourself but get it done.

Remember the vegetable garden out back that's weedy, wild, and overgrown for lack of attention? Get out there and tend it, and then enjoy the fruits and vegetables of your labors. Eating food you've grown yourself is uniquely satisfying— especially for urban types. Or try an ornamental garden instead.

Many nurseries and discount home and garden centers have knowledgeable staff and often can refer you to contractors to help with planning and executing your dream project.

If the physical labor of your project is too demanding for your health and well-being, act as your own contractor and oversee the work or just watch as others put it together. Then beam with pride at the accomplishment.

Reality Check:
As with anything requiring outside assistance or guidance, always work with and buy from reputable organizations. Ask for references and then talk to them. Also check out any potential contractor or business with your local Better Business Bureau or the BBB online before any money changes hands.

What It Takes to Get There:
www.doityourself.com; www.homestore.com; www.hgtv.com; www.builderdirectory.com; www.homedepot.com; www.bbbonline.com; www.lowes.com; www.thisoldhouse.com.

Cost: Varies; the cheapest option seldom turns out to be the best.

Top left: A choir may be your ticket to camaraderie. Left: Ski resorts may need your help on their ski patrols.
Above: Retirement is prime time for Mr. and Mrs. Fix-It, Remodel-It, or Repair-It.

Fun

22 Root for the Home Team
Buy Season Tickets, Get Involved, and Volunteer

Take your pick of professional, college, amateur, intramural, or high school sports. Teams, even professional ones, don't exist without your support, and getting involved offers unique possibilities for enjoyment.

Consider professional football teams. The fans they breed are in a league of their own. Where else can a person paint his or her face blue, red, or green, wear a barrel in below-zero weather, and be accepted without question?

We're not necessarily advocating that you dress up like a rooster for the next game, but the ways to show your team spirit are limited only by your imagination. Teams at every level need help, from manning the concession stand to soliciting advertising for the team programs. Your time, talents, and services can make a difference.

Reality Check:
Smaller teams count on volunteers, and even the big guys may need your help. Don't be discouraged if no one wants your time. Be persistent. In the interim, master the art of tailgating or team parties, rally a fan club (formal or otherwise), and have fun.

What It Takes to Get There:

That depends on the sport, your team, and the game.

Cost: The price of a ticket; certain cable and Web broadcasts are on demand for a fee or free depending on the event.

www.seniorolympics.org; www.nsga.com; www.seniorjournal.com, click on health and fitness; www.active.com.

Cost: Free and up, depending on your goals.

23 Go for the Gold
Improve Your Game

Set your sights on perfecting your serve, putt, volley, stroke, or form. Concentrate on becoming an expert at a favorite sport or sports. Lower your golf handicap. Shave seconds off that ski run or lap swim. Speed up that tennis serve and pair it with a wicked backhand.

Get that coach or take those lessons you've always talked about. You might be surprised at how good you can get. An extra perk: Active retirees generally are healthier retirees. Forget wasting away in a lounger all day in front of the TV. Go for it!

Proficiency at any sport takes commitment, hours of practice, and plenty of sweat, even if your sport happens to be croquet or table tennis. But the effort will be worth the satisfaction, especially if an opponent happens to be a cocky youngster!

Reality Check:
Age does have its limitations, so before starting any sport or training program, check with your doctor first. Also, remember that your peak performance won't be the same at 70 as it was at 17.

24 Picture This
Take Up Photography

Chronicle the world, life, and loved ones from a different angle. Get behind the lens of a camera. We've all grown up taking pictures. And, one or two almost always turn out pretty well. But wouldn't it be great if nearly every image was a standout? They can be, with a little extra time and professional direction.

Start by studying great pictures and then take a photography course from a community college, senior center, local organization, or even a camera shop. Learn about the nuances of light, subject matter, backgrounds, and foregrounds. Understand how to maximize the ability of your camera. Many stores offer free lessons with a camera purchase.

Today's digital cameras add a new dimension to picture taking, and amateurs armed with a PC can enhance images like a professional. Why not shoot for a spread in *National Geographic*?

Left: Football offers plenty of options for fans and volunteers alike. Top: Nothing says you still can't excel in your sport. Right: Check out life through the lens of a camera.

Snap your loved ones, chronicle your travels or a special event, or simply find the pictures in the world around you.

Reality Check:
You may not feel you have a good photographic eye, but nearly everyone can improve his or her picture-taking ability.

What It Takes to Get There:
www.canon.com; www.nationalgeographic.com; www.nikon.com; www.poyi.org.

Cost: Free and up.

25 Delectable Collectibles
Start a Collection and Become an Authority

For the true collector, successful collecting becomes a passion that drives an insatiable appetite to learn as much as possible about the chosen subject. Such collectors, in turn, often become experts who advise others.

If you're a beginner, why not give antiques a try— more specifically English, German, or French porcelain; Staffordshire figurines; milk glass; 19th century lithographs; or Early American pewter.

Are you a Coca-Cola fan? That brand's namesake paraphernalia is a favorite among collectors. What about a circa 1962 Coke machine or those infamous giant Coca-Cola bottle-cap signs? You didn't think twice about them as a child, but now they bring back a flood of memories. Do you still have that Barbie doll? If it's in the original box, you could have a gold mine.

And, of course, the baseball trading cards that your mom tossed out when you went to college would be worth a fortune now.

The perks of collecting range from new friendships to learning and traveling and, most of all, enjoying your collection.

Reality Check:
Without really trying, you or your heirs may end up making money courtesy of your collection.

What It Takes to Get There:
www.awsmfind.com, then click on Collectibles; http://collectibles.about.com, then click on Collector Resources.

Cost: Inexpensive to very expensive.

26 Dig for Your Roots
Trace Your Family's Genealogy

Everyone knows that tracing a family tree can satisfy curiosity about where your ancestors came from. But it also can tell a great deal about who you are. After all, through our genes we carry our parents with us, just as our parents carried their parents, and so on.

How did your family get where it is today? Where did your ancestors come from and why did they leave? Many current generations can't answer those simple questions. You may remember that the family came to Missouri in a covered wagon

Above: Shop for goodies at Black Creek Pioneer Village, Toronto, Ontario, Canada. Top right: Photos, like this one of children in Neosho, Missouri, circa 1900, provide links to the past. Right: Spiff up that old Mustang. Don't forget a safety check, too.

in 1878, or that Great-Great-Aunt Jo had a son, Great-Uncle Harry, who no one ever mentions, but who will remember after you die?

Tracing a family genealogy is a legacy for your children, grandchildren, and great-grandchildren. Write it down and create a true book of life. No matter how insignificant something sounds to you today, it may be invaluable to future generations.

Reality Check:
Be careful of online sales pitches that claim an organization will help trace your roots if you "send $19.95!" Verify credentials and reputation first.

What It Takes to Get There:
Check with local and national historical societies, public libraries, and national and international religious, ethnic, and cultural genealogy groups; www.genealogytoday.com; name searches on favorite search engines.

Cost: Depends on complexity of search.

27 Real Wheels
Find and Restore a Vintage Car

That hot car you always wanted as a teenager but couldn't afford—or that your mom and dad wouldn't let you have—is finally within reach. Think 1965 Mustang convertible or 1967 Corvette Stingray. Try your restorative prowess on a Pierce-Arrow, Packard, Triumph, or Nash.

Keep in mind, however, that restoring an old car might not be as easy—or as inexpensive—as you might think. What happens if something breaks? Where will you find the parts to fix it? Those answers can be elusive as well as costly. Garages and storage units are full of half-assembled cars collecting dust instead of fulfilling dreams. Nonetheless, you can cruise to glory. All you have to do is find your dreamboat, buy it, and then restore it.

For unique fun, if your vehicle is 1960 or earlier, join other like-minded enthusiasts and run the Great Race, an annual 4,000-mile transcontinental odyssey.

Reality Check:
Approach this pastime with caution or else your cash-guzzling relic could end up a family sore spot.

What It Takes to Get There:
Many options are available, including http://vintagecars.about.com, with lots of links; www.autoindiamart.com; www.autoweek.com; www.classiccar.com; www.greatrace.com; Antique Automobile Club of America, www.aaca.org.

Cost: That's up to you. The entry fee for the Great Race is $5,000.

Social

28 Deal Yourself In
Card Clubs Run the Gamut

Choose your game—bridge, poker, mahjong, pinochle, even old maid—and join an existing club or start your own. Card clubs are a great way to meet and enjoy your peers, especially if you're not as mobile as you once were. For excitement, mix it up with younger members.

Take the games seriously, hone your skill, and end up in international competitions. Or play simply for fun and friendship. Senior organizations as well as country clubs, social clubs, business clubs, and more offer card-playing groups. Neighborhood associations have clubs, too.

Reality Check:
Cardplaying can be a great way to socialize and meet people.

What It Takes to Get There:
www.greatbridgelinks.com/gblTOUR;
www.pokerpages.com.

Cost: Less than $1 and up, depending on where you buy your cards, lessons, poker chips, and more.

29 Privileges of Membership
Join a Club or Senior Center

Learn about the world or the town down the road; attend the theater or movies; prepare and eat gourmet cuisine; choose solid investments; read the latest bestseller; sing oldies; or simply socialize. If something is of interest to you, odds are that others have formed a club to share that interest. If you can't find the club you're seeking in your area, start one.

Clubs are a wonderful way to do what you enjoy with people you enjoy, and all in a positive environment. Clubs also offer the opportunity to travel. Think about the book club that takes a junket to London to see a play, or the investment club that heads across country to check out a particular company up close. Many clubs branch out from their original purpose to try something new just because the members like each other and get along so well. And don't forget: as a club member, you'll probably host a get-together, which is the perfect excuse for a party.

You don't have to spend your older years in solitude. Pursue your interests and get involved.

Reality Check:
Don't use "I don't drive" as an excuse not to join a club. Members generally are happy to help others who can't drive or don't want to.

What It Takes to Get There:

National Association of Investors Corporation, www.betterinvesting.org; American Association of Individual Investors, www.aaii.org; check with local senior centers and organizations.

Cost: Dues, depending on the club, and cost, if any, of the activity.

Talk to the World
Ham It Up with Amateur Radio

This may be the era of downloads and chat rooms, but to a devoted group of hams an evening with an earful of static and chatter beats time online any day or night.

The Information Age hasn't dampened the enthusiasm that people of all ages worldwide have for amateur radio. Ham operators, with their two-way radios, play a major role in emergency and search and rescue communications, too.

If you think it's old-fashioned, think again. Amateur radio has gone high-tech and handheld. Hams keep in touch via radio and use their online connections to provide more ways to communicate and get the word out.

Talk to your neighbor down the street, a friend across the world, or even an astronaut in space.

Build your own set or buy one. It's up to you. And remember, you never know who you will end up chatting with tomorrow.

Reality Check:
Licensing, including written examinations, is required for use.

What It Takes to Get There:

American Radio Relay League, the National Association for Amateur Radio, www.arrl.org; Amateur Radio Disaster Services, www.ares.org; Federal Trade Commission, www.ftc.gov, click on For Consumers and follow the links.

Cost: The sky is the limit.

Top left: Turn your card club meeting into a party. Top above: Clubs are a great way to socialize.
Above: Peggy Sue Rackham, right, with Doug Hutton, answered her call as an amateur radio operator.

Personal Growth and Self-Development

A sound mind in a sound body is your ticket to a successful retirement. Make the most of your opportunities to stay physically, mentally, and spiritually fit.

Mental Challenge

31 A Major Undertaking
Go Back to School

Use retirement as an opportunity to expand your mind. Get bitten anew by the academic bug and return to your old major. If you've never been to college, this is your chance. If it's your second time around, you'll relax and enjoy college more without the pressure to build a successful life that you may have felt starting out.

Revisit your old major or try something new. Finish an elusive degree, pursue a new one, or simply audit a course or two for the joy of learning. Classes can be virtual or otherwise. Grades often are optional. (You'll probably get all As now that a gradepoint average doesn't really matter!) Some institutions even allow seniors and retirees to attend classes for free.

Educational options abound at colleges, community colleges, universities, online learning institutions, and free universities. Special sessions at Florida-based Senior Summer School, for example, address a number of topics and are held at eight different campuses in North America.

Reality Check:
Always check the accreditation and legitimacy of any institution or program before paying tuition.

What It Takes to Get There:
Check individual institutions' Web sites;
www.collegeboard.com; www.xap.com;
Council for Higher Education Accreditation,
www.chea.org; Senior Summer School,
www.seniorsummerschool.com; www.elderhostel.org.

Cost: Brace yourself for stratospheric increases. One year, tuition only, at UCLA, is about $14,700 to $17,300; Bowdoin College, Brunswick, Maine, about $30,950; Colorado Christian University, Lakewood, Colorado, $350/credit hour; Senior Summer School, about $1,300 to $4,500/session.

32 Avoid the Unspeakable
Learn Another Language

Parlez-vous français? Sprechen sie deutsch? ¿Habla usted español? What about Russian, Japanese, Swahili, Mandarin, Vietnamese, or any other language?

Double your fluency and build neural pathways in your brain by learning another language. You'll gain insight into another country's culture as you do.

If world travel is in your retirement plans, learning the language of your planned destination enhances enjoyment of your trip and comes in

Left: Consider earning an advanced degree or honors. Above: Learning the language of the place or places you plan to visit adds to the enjoyment of your travel.

handy, especially if the language uses an entirely different alphabet.

Foreign-language study options range from private, in-your-home instruction to virtual and in-school classrooms, self-administered courses, and travel/study. Take a language-learning holiday in the country of your choice; try fast-track learning at home; rely on software, tapes, and CDs; or turn to colleges and universities or cultural and heritage centers in your community. If you're looking for private instruction, try posting notes on school bulletin boards.

Reality Check:

Despite what many Americans assume, English is not the universal language, and many places don't post international symbols. It's tough when you're seeking the entrance and wind up at the exit because you can't decipher the signs.

What It Takes to Get There:

Berlitz, www.berlitz.com;
Fairfield Language Technologies/Rosetta Stone Language Software, www.rosettastone.com;
Internet Course Finders/Language-Learning.net, www.language-learning.net;
www.foreignlanguagehome.com,
search tool by country; www.abroadlanguages.com.

Cost: Lessons vary by institution, location, and type, with scholarships often available; software, about $330 for Spanish (Rosetta Stone); virtual classroom, 30 semiprivate lessons, about $800 (Berlitz).

33 Life-Saving Skills
Get Certified in First Aid and CPR

You may never face a life-threatening emergency, but what if you do? You could save a life or, at the very least, make a big difference by learning cardiopulmonary resuscitation (CPR) and first-aid skills.

Even if you think you know what to do in an emergency, brush up on your technique and skills with a formal CPR and first-aid course. They're available online and in person from a variety of organizations, ranging from the Red Cross to your local community or senior center, hospitals and medical centers, local YMCAs, community colleges, and nearby schools.

You literally will rest easier if you know that you can handle an emergency, especially if you spend time or live with someone in poor health. An added bonus: you'll feel better equipped to babysit your grandchildren.

Reality Check:

Taking a quick course for a small price isn't much sacrifice for being able to help someone in need, possibly even a spouse or loved one.

What It Takes to Get There:

Red Cross, www.redcross.org; www.firstaidweb.com; www.emergencyuniversity.com.

Cost: CPR courses range from free online (without a formal certificate) to less than $100.

34 Retire with Rhythm
Dance through Retirement

Stay fit, socialize, and keep the beat with dance lessons. The possibilities are endless: swing, ballroom, salsa, ballet, hip-hop, jazz, modern, folk, rock and roll, tap. Break dancing, however, may be out of your league.

Still, don't automatically reject any particular dance form because of physical limitations. Think creatively. A tapper can sit, a ballerina can lean, and a wheelchair can twirl.

Find the right teacher and then get into the routine. No prior experience required. Go solo and grab a partner or take your honey with you. Try private or group lessons. Join a dance club and then dance your way through retirement.

Reality Check:
Dance, like any exercise, can be strenuous, so check with your doctor before getting started.

What It Takes to Get There:
www.ballroomdancers.com; Imperial Society of Teachers of Dancing, www.istd.org; AccessDance Network, www.accessdance.com; many Web sites offer dance videos.

Cost: Varies by type of dance and instructor; some places offer free instruction.

35 Back in the Saddle Again
Learn to Ride a Horse

Horseback riding remains a unique opportunity to connect with a 1,000-pound animal. That animal may be ten times your weight, but it works for you and with you, and the partnership is an incredible experience.

Enjoy the freedom of galloping across an open field, or the thrill of working in tandem with your equine to score a goal at polo or perform the perfect routine in the ring. Experience nature atop a horse, and you may end up jumping a creek, galloping with deer, or enjoying the serenity of a lazy river.

For real adventure, get your in-the-saddle experience at a dude ranch. Most have seniors and/or adult-only sessions. Some are quite rustic. You can have a week to yourself with the staff at The Fort Ranch in rural Nevada. Other ranches, like the C Lazy U in Colorado, offer more upscale amenities.

Left: A volunteer with the Corporation for National and Community Service shares her skills with others.
Top: Keep in step with dance. Above right: Try a dude ranch vacation to get a taste of the Old West.

Reality Check:

Horses are large, lovable, and unpredictable. Never take them for granted and make sure your riding skills are a match for your mount.

What It Takes to Get There:

www.classicaldressage.co.uk;
North American Riding for the Handicapped Association, www.narha.org; http://gorp.away.com, click on Activities and then Horseback;
The Dude Ranchers' Association,
www.duderanch.org; C Lazy U, www.clazyu.com;
American Riding Instructors Association,
www.riding-instructor.com; U.S. Equestrian Federation, www.usef.org;
U.S. Polo Association, www.us-polo.org.

Cost: Riding lessons are about $35 to $45/hour; dude ranch, about $1,000 to $3,700/week, including horse.

36 Safety Behind the Wheel
Take Driver Safety

Road conditions, other drivers, and inclement weather aren't the only hazards drivers face, especially as they age. Some medications may affect your driving ability. Also, reflexes can slow as people age, and vision and hearing may not be as sharp as they used to be.

All these things can manifest themselves when you get behind the wheel of a vehicle. These issues require honest assessments on your part because lives—including your own—could be at stake. Better still, don't fret the what-ifs; instead, brush up on your driving prowess with a driver safety course. Plenty of local, national, and international organizations and groups, including AARP, offer driver safety and other practical for-the-road courses.

If you think a driving refresher course is for the other guy or if you're reluctant to take such a course, check out AARP's Driving IQ test online. You may be surprised at the results. Also check out the AAA Foundation for Traffic Safety's Web site on senior driver safety.

Reality Check:

Everyone can benefit from a driving refresher course occasionally. AARP's program is geared to age 50 and up, but it's open to others, too.

What It Takes to Get There:

www.aarp.org, type in driver safety and follow the links; www.seniordrivers.org; www.seniorsite.com and follow the links.

Cost: AARP's course is about $10.

37 Food for Thought
Improve Your Culinary Skills

How to boil water may not be an issue, but perfecting meringue or slicing sushi could matter a great deal to your taste buds and enjoyment of food. Ditto for making paella on the grill or concocting the ultimate barbecue sauce. Even learning the correct way to sharpen a knife or open a springform pan can be eye-opening and disaster-averting!

Why not get a taste of how to do all this—and much more—the proper way? Sign up for a local or long-distance cooking class. Options range from formal cooking schools—some on location in Europe—to occasional classes from gourmet and kitchen retailers, private lessons, TV chefs, and even informal get-togethers with friends and neighbors.

More options:

- Form or join a cooking club. Meet once a month and learn something new at every get-together.

- Get hot tips from participants at food festivals and cooking contests.

- Ask food sellers for their favorite recipes and then try them out at home.

- Read new and different cookbooks and then experiment.

Reality Check:
If you decide to experiment, always keep peanut butter, jelly, and antacid handy.

What It Takes to Get There:

Check with local specialty shops and restaurants; Culinary Ed, www.culinaryed.com; www.starchefs.com; www.foodnetwork.com; www.foodandwine.com; The International Kitchen, www.theinternationalkitchen.com.

Cost: Free and up; five days at the Villa d'Este on Lake Como in Italy, about $2,500 to $2,750.

38 Spread Your Wings
Learn to Fly

Unlock the mystery of flight for yourself. The key is as near as your neighborhood flight instructor. A word of warning, however: Flying high in the sky can be an addictive pastime. Once you've tried it, you'll never want to stop.

Left: The nonprofit AAA Foundation for Traffic Safety offers much helpful information for seniors.
Above: Tasting your culinary creation is half the fun of cooking.

Lessons are fun, the people are interesting, and you'll learn about much more than how to fly a plane, including weather, physics, and how and why a plane stays aloft.

Lessons are available across the country. Unfortunately, from a financial point of view, one or two aren't enough to earn a pilot certification. The Federal Aviation Administration has strict requirements for air time and written examination. It's estimated that it takes, on average, 50 hours of instruction and 60 hours of flight time to earn your wings. The cost adds up quickly.

Some training facilities have low-cost introductory flights to help potential students decide whether to invest the time and money in flight training.

Reality Check:
A medical certification from a Federal Aviation Administration authorized examiner is required to fly solo. The FAA suggests getting it up front.

What It Takes to Get There:

FAA, www.faa.gov;
www.aviationschoolsonline.com;
www.bestaviationsites.com;
Universal Information eXchange, http://u-i-x.com;
www.flyairorlando.com.

Cost: Variable, depends on aircraft, instructor, and school; FAA numbers, around $45/hour for an instructor and about $100/hour for a typical four-seater plane. Total cost can run about $5,500 and up.

39 Safely Sail Away
Take a Boater Safety Course

Sure, it's easy to just haul up the anchor on your boat and sail away. But are you current on the latest boating-safety issues? Are you aware of the very real dangers of carbon-monoxide poisoning on a boat? How good a navigator are you? Do you know how to read depth charts well enough to avoid a sandbar? Do you know procedures for a water emergency?

With more than 17.5 million boats in the United States (2004 estimate from the National Marine Manufacturing Association), even the casual boater needs to know the basics or risk real danger in the event of a problem.

Safety courses are available online, in book form, and in person through various agencies and organizations. So brush up and head out for a safer, more enjoyable time on the water. Earn a transport certification from the U.S. Coast Guard and pilot charters on your own vacations.

Reality Check:
In 2003, more than 5,400 boating accidents occurred with more than 700 deaths, according to U.S. Coast Guard statistics. Factors contributing to the accidents include operator inattention and inexperience, carelessness/reckless operation, and excessive speed.

Reality Check:
Almost all judicial proceedings are open to the public. But a judge can order closed hearings or meet in chambers with the parties involved.

What It Takes to Get There:

www.nolo.com, click on Rights and Disputes, then Criminal Law; www.talkjustice.com; American Bar Association, www.abanet.org; www.decisionquest.com.

Cost: Admission is free.

What It Takes to Get There:

Boat Owners Association of the United States, www.boatus.com; U.S. Coast Guard Office of Boating Safety, www.uscgboating.org; www.commanderbob.com; www.seaschool.com; National Marine Manufacturers Association, www.nmma.org.

Cost: Approximately $20 and up, depending on the course.

40 Courtroom Drama
Watch a Trial

View the alternately fascinating and frustrating world of America's justice system up close. See its strengths and weakness firsthand. A trial is the ultimate reality show—players reap real rewards and suffer real consequences.

Sit in on a murder, kidnapping, or medical malpractice case. A number of organizations count on volunteers to monitor certain court proceedings for rights violations. Research what happens in a trial in general (a good place to start is the American Bar Association), then select a courtroom, pick a seat, and listen for yourself. Draw your own conclusions from the testimony and evidence.

Above left: Learn the nuts and bolts of flying. Top: Safety is key to boating fun. Above: Sit in on a trial and decide for yourself a defendant's guilt or innocence.

Physical Fitness

41 Fit for Life

Think Healthy Food and Good Exercise

If you're overweight, flabby, or even too thin, consider tuning up your body. Not only will you look and feel better, but you'll also have more energy for those activities you want to do but can't because of your size, health, or attitude.

Join a fitness club or organization, local or otherwise. Consider a stay at a health or fitness spa or get involved in a regular yoga program. Get going on that exercise regimen you plan every New Year's but never get around to doing. Exercise does not have to be complicated. Studies show that even regular walking benefits your heart. So does exercise like yoga, aerobics, dancing, and more.

Take a hike to the mailbox or the park. The next time you're at the mall, park your car a little farther from the entrance. Better yet, grab a friend or two and do some "mall walking." Forgo the golf cart and walk those 9 or even 18 holes. Swimming is another wonderful aerobic exercise for older individuals and seniors that is low impact and low stress to boot. Many local groups offer classes tailored to older people, and most pools offer adult swim time or lap-only lanes. Don't just take your grandchild to the pool. Put on your suit and jump in with him or her! Consider a yoga class or try it on your own. The exercises stretch muscles, loosen joints, and add to your overall relaxation.

Check out the American Heart Association for more information on these and other ways to get and stay fit.

Reality Check:

Consult with your doctor before getting started.

What It Takes to Get There:

http://www.americanheart.org; www.50plus.org; www.ediet.com; www.weightwatchers.com; www.active.com; www.healthclubs.com; www.justmove.org.

Cost: Free and up.

The New You
Go for That Makeover

Tired of looking at the same "you" in the mirror? Think about a makeover. Try a visit to your favorite cosmetics counter for its version of the new you. Try a new hairstyle or hair color if the mood suits you, and don't overlook a wardrobe revamp to boost a sagging self-image.

Cosmetic surgery may be another more serious option, one that has its supporters and detractors. Reality shows may glamorize it; others reject it. Many procedures are quite costly and rarely covered by typical health insurance policies.

Whether to get a nip, tuck, lift, or injection ultimately is your decision. Many procedures are done on an outpatient basis or involve only a short hospital stay. If you're considering cosmetic surgery, experts recommend that you thoroughly check out the procedure, its risks and its benefits before undergoing the knife or laser. Some procedures are far less drastic than others. Rather than getting a face-lift, Botox or a collagen injection might provide just the boost you need. As with any medical procedure, thoroughly check out the credentials and medical reputation of the surgeon you're considering.

Everyone shows his or her age eventually. Some prefer to conceal it as long as possible. You certainly don't need plastic surgery to enjoy retirement, but if you've always wanted to make a physical change as opposed to a cosmetic one and haven't done so, retirement provides the perfect opportunity. An alternative first step: Try a makeup, hair, and wardrobe makeover.

Reality Check:

Some procedures are relatively painless, others more lengthy and sometimes painful.

What It Takes to Get There:

Visit your favorite makeup counter or hairdresser. For medical procedures, American Society of Plastic Surgeons, www.plasticsurgery.org; Canadian Academy of Facial Plastic Reconstructive Surgery, www.facialcosmeticsurgery.org; American Academy of Cosmetic Surgery, www.cosmeticsurgery.org; American Academy of Facial Plastic and Reconstructive Surgery, www.aafprs.org; www.smartplasticsurgery.com.

Cost: Varies; a haircut under $50; cosmetic makeover, free at some stores; medical procedures vary, about $400 for Botox injections; about $8,500 for face-lift (according to SmartPlasticSurgery.com).

Top left: Regular exercise, including biking, pays health dividends. Above: If you're thinking about a new look, you have plenty of options.

Spiritual Wellness

43 Follow Your Faith
Get Involved in a Religious Group

Many people approaching their later years want to know more about the God of their understanding and experience. Becoming more involved with your church, synagogue, mosque, or temple can help you grow spiritually. Most places of worship offer a variety of outreach and faith-formation groups where you can help others as well as find solid direction, solace, and companionship. Being involved in such a group can be truly comforting, especially when dealing with catastrophic illness or the loss of a loved one.

If you haven't had any religious affiliation in the past, you may want to think about one for the future. People who shy away from organized religion might consider joining or forming a neighborhood prayer or study group. Spiritual options for the nondenominational include starting a group that studies the world's religions, for example, or joining an organization devoted to world peace.

Reality Check:

If you opt not to join a church, synagogue, mosque, or temple, it's a good idea to fill out a funeral directive that lets family and loved ones know how, in the absence of familiar clergy, you would like your eventual funeral handled. Typically, clergy lead the services.

What It Takes to Get There:

Check your local telephone books, the Web, and church directories.

Cost: Varies depending on the religion, customs, and specific church, synagogue, mosque, or temple. For many religious institutions, contributions are voluntary, though encouraged.

Revive Your Soul

Take a Spiritual Retreat

Spend a long weekend, a few days, a week, or longer at a monastery or retreat to rejuvenate and recharge your body and soul. Go for the serenity, peace, or religious experience. Whatever the reason, a retreat is a welcome oasis of calm amid the stresses of everyday life.

Monasteries often offer retreats on a specific topic with speakers and workshops, or you can go solo and spend unstructured time the way you wish. Guest rooms tend to be reasonably priced, but some are more comfortable than others. Guests on retreats often may dine with the monks and attend services; group retreats usually involve shared meals and activities.

Some retreats—especially the secular ones—offer guests a bit more luxury, even to the point of being spalike. While some places tend to be trendy, others are more serious respites where one explores aspects of one's inner life and strives for serenity and inner peace. Some organizations also offer yoga retreats.

Reality Check:

Verify the reputation and background of any group or place before booking your getaway.

What It Takes to Get There:

Use the keywords *monastery, retreat,* and *yoga* and search the Web, and then choose your preference; alternatively, www.retreatsonline.com; www.whereintheworld.co.uk, click on Spiritual Journeys.

Cost: Inexpensive to high-ticket, depending on your choices.

Left: A church in Shigawake, Quebec, Canada, stands as a symbol of faith for many. Above: A spiritual getaway truly can refresh your mind, body, and soul.

Finding Your Way Home

Wherever your roots — even if they're mobile — this is your opportunity to find and make the home you've always wanted.

45 Stay Home
Don't Move

Retirement does not necessarily mean moving to a different home. If you're satisfied with where you are and your home "fits," then stay put and avoid the hassle of pulling up roots.

Determining whether you and your home are still a good fit, however, requires a realistic and honest analysis of whether you're willing and able to handle the responsibilities of that home. Keep in mind that your home may be great now but could become a burden later. For that reason, some retirees move soon after retirement to allow them to actively make new friends and develop support groups in their new community.

Don't overlook the possibility of modifying or remodeling your current home now for ease of living later. Consider adding universal design features that include options like no-step entry, wider doorways and hallways, extra floor space, and more. (Learn more about universal design online at www.aarp.org).

The best advice: Don't automatically reject any move, and don't rule one out later.

Reality Check:
Retirees often wait too long to give up a big house and move to more manageable living quarters. The result: They often end up unhappy and friendless in a strange place, which might even include assisted living or a nursing home.

What It Takes to Get There:

http://seniorliving.about.com; www.wheretoretire.com; U.S. Department of Housing and Urban Development, www.hud.gov/consumer; www.seniorresource.com.

Cost: Remodeling costs vary; new bathroom tile, about $300; handrail, several dollars and up.

46 Downsize
Move to a Smaller Home

If you don't need or want to maintain a large home, think about downsizing instead. But moving to a smaller home won't automatically lower your household expenses and boost your savings. If you trade down in size but up in amenities, your cost of living might actually increase.

Costs aside, a trade down will cut your workload and responsibilities. Choosing a smaller home, condominium, patio home, or the like will cut down on big yards to mow and long driveways to clear of snow. Or if you're trudging up and down the stairs in a multilevel home right now, think how easy a ranch-style or one-story condo will be when you have difficulty getting around.

Left: You must decide if your current home is a good fit for you. Above right: Retirement could be the opportunity to move into a custom-built home of your dreams.

Trading down offers a great opportunity to live in your dream home on a smaller, more manageable scale for today and the future.

Reality Check:
Plan for the future for worry-free living today and tomorrow.

What It Takes to Get There:

HSH Associates, www.hsh.com, click on Library; http://rpsrelocation.com; Administration on Aging, www.aoa.gov, then click on Elders and Families, then Housing; www.seniortransitionsnw.com.

47 A Change of Culture
Relocate across Town or across the World

In retirement, you have the freedom to move to a neighboring street or state, a foreign country, a quiet tropical island, a thriving metropolis, or a small town. The world is your oyster!

Don't automatically reject moving to a retirement community, either. Think seriously about the options and advantages of living among people who often share similar interests and lifestyles. Today's retirement communities range from active

over-55 centers for golf, tennis, nature, and socializing on one end to assisted living and full-time nursing care at the other.

Another option is the expatriate life. Some towns in Mexico are homes away from home, where your new neighbors could be from your old hometown. Many places in the Caribbean and cities like Jerusalem and Paris are much the same.

Some people opt to sell their homes and start completely over in a new location. Others keep both their old home and new. Not certain you're ready to sever local ties? Look into exchanging homes with someone who lives in the locale you're considering.

Reality Check:
Thoroughly check out any option you're considering.

What It Takes to Get There:

www.retirmenthomes.com; www.delwebb.com; www.retirenet.com. Home swaps: HomeLink International, www.swapnow.com; www.intervac-online.com; www.seniorshomeexchange.com.

Cost: Depends on your choices; home exchanges often include use of a vehicle.

48 Off the Beaten Track
Pursue a Community Lifestyle

One of the great things about retirement is that you get to choose your lifestyle. With the kids grown and fewer social obligations to fulfill, you can explore some less traditional housing options.

Above: You could make your next home in Villefranche or other points in France. Top right: Residents at Munksgaard Senior Cohousing, Roskilde, Denmark, dine together. Right: A vacation home provides a getaway.

Perhaps the participative nature of cohousing, the egalitarian aspect of a commune, the freedom of a naturist, or another lifestyle out of the mainstream fits your tastes. All these and more are viable options if you so choose.

Cohousing is a cooperative community where residents own their private homes or apartments but also share extensive facilities that usually include a common area or building. There's no shared economy as in a commune, but community decisions generally are by consensus.

More communal in nature than cohousing are communes and intentional communities. A kibbutz, for example, is a form of communal living. So are dozens of egalitarian communities worldwide, whether they're in rural Israel, suburban St. Louis, or urban Seattle. Some are secular in nature, and some are based simply on shared interests.

Reality Check:
Before making any commitment to a group, thoroughly check its references, credentials, and reputation.

What It Takes to Get There:
Cohousing Association of the United States, www.cohousing.org; Intentional Communities, www.ic.org; Global Ecovillage Network, http://gen.ecovillage.org; The Federation of Egalitarian Communities, http://thefec.org; International Communes Desk, www.communa.org; Naturist Society, www.naturistsociety.com; American Association for Nude Recreation, www.aanr.com.

Cost: Depends on your choices.

Add a Castle
Buy a Second Home

Eliminate those hassles over where to go for the weekend, the week, or the winter by purchasing a second home. Buy a share, as in time-share or fractional ownership, or the whole kit and caboodle.

Own a villa in Italy or a cabin on the lake, a condo in California or a mansion in the Adirondacks. Even a trailer in the woods could qualify as a vacation retreat. Rent it out or keep it for yourself.

People often buy second homes with the expectation of eventually turning them into permanent residences.

Whatever your choice, proceed with caution. Second homes have tax and other financial ramifications.

Reality Check:
Be careful of scams. Before committing any money, check references and reputations, and also check with the area Better Business Bureau.

What It Takes to Get There:
www.escapehomes.com;
www.seniorshomeexchange.com;
www.bankrate.com.

Cost: That's up to you.

50 Live on and off the Land
Buy a Farm or Winery

Spend a bundle for a Napa Valley vineyard or get a deal on some acreage in Wyoming. With the right planning, joining the landed gentry can become an achievable dream.

If living on the land appeals to you but hard labor does not, look at creative ways to cut the workload or eliminate it altogether. Buy a farm with an already established tenant farmer, for example. Or if you've fallen in love with a small vegetable or fruit farm, consider Pick Your Own as a way to limit harvesting chores.

With a winery, the attraction may be simply to own a beautiful property and be involved with making and enjoying fine wine. Others can handle the labor, including the actual winemaking.

Reality Check:

Owning a farm or winery involves a special kind of lifestyle commitment as well as knowledge of the product or crop, its production cycle, related sales and marketing, and overall economics. Pay particular attention to water rights. The right to use water on your property is not automatic in some parts of the country.

What It Takes to Get There:

National Family Farm Coalition, www.nffc.net; www.pickyourown.org; http://ecoop.netsville.com; National Farmers Union, www.nfu.org; www.wineryxrealestate.com; Cascade Foothills Farmland Association, www.visitwashingtonfarms.com.

Cost: Not inexpensive.

51 Share Some School Spirit
Move to a College Town

Think about making a new home amid the intelligentsia of Ann Arbor, Michigan (University of Michigan); the mountains of Boulder, Colorado (University of Colorado); the fall foliage of Hamilton, New York (Colgate University); the spirit of Auburn, Alabama (Auburn University); the quaintness of Oxford, Ohio (Miami University); or the sensory stimuli of myriad academic institutions—including your alma mater. Academia knows no bounds.

Moving to a college town can mean unlimited intellectual stimulation and access to the arts while cheering for the home team and mingling with tomorrow's leaders.

Go for the big-city, inner-city campus life or enroll in school full-time in pursuit of a degree, advanced or otherwise.

Reality Check:

You can live the dream. No age limits; class attendance optional.

What It Takes to Get There:

Visit Web sites of specific colleges and universities, then click on information about campus life. Alternatively, pick up a catalog of universities and colleges, or visit www.collegeboard.com and click on College Matchmaker.

Cost: That depends on your lifestyle and choices.

52 Packaged Move
Move to a Manufactured Home

Imagine a home as a package that you can pick up and move (albeit with some difficulty) if and when the spirit moves you. And it's not a cramped RV!

Welcome to the world of manufactured homes that include factory-built permanent and mobile homes. This popular housing option can downsize your space, responsibility, and expenses. Retirees often cash in on the equity of their family residence in a northern clime, for instance, and then move someplace warmer and buy a much less expensive manufactured home.

Going manufactured requires far less commitment than buying a site-built home, and if you discover you don't like your new location, you can easily move elsewhere.

Reality Check:

Mobile-home living today isn't what it used to be. If you're not sure the lifestyle is for you, consider a vacation rental first.

What It Takes to Get There:

Manufactured Housing Institute, www.manufacturedhousing.org; HUD, www.hud.gov; Manufactured Housing Global Network, www.mfdhousing.com.

Cost: Average sales price, about $58,000.

Left: Farm life holds special appeal for many people. Top: The ambiance of a college town is tough to match.
Above: Today's manufactured homes aren't the cramped quarters of yesterday.

Once (or Twice) in a Lifetime Adventures

Wanderlust and adrenaline can kick in no matter your age, situation, or the challenge. Dream it; plan it; do it.

Big Times

53 Go Hog Wild
Roar across America on a Motorcycle

Motorcyclists take the lure of the open road to heart. Riding coast to coast qualifies as taking the sport to the max—"easy rider" on steroids. It's also a pipe dream of young and old, and both men and women. Those who have done it talk of the challenge and the accomplishment, and they marvel at the open air, new friendships, and unparalleled beauty of America.

If you're not quite ready for a trip from Kennebunkport (Maine) to Los Angeles, an alternative with plenty of saddle time is the annual Mother Road Rally, a 2,448-mile ride every June along historic Route 66. (Many participants don't ride the entire way!)

UltimateVroom:
Head to Sturgis, South Dakota, for the annual Black Hills Motor Classic every summer.

Reality Check:
Forget the oldfangled notion that bikers mean trouble. The weekend and cross-country enthusiasts you meet on the road are more likely to be moms and pops, CEOs, and MDs than gang members and deadbeats.

What It Takes to Get There:
Check out www.bikersites.com for a searchable index of services and providers; www.motorcity.net; www.hhjm.com, for information on the Mother Road Rally; Christian Motorcyclists Association, www.cmausa.org; www.sturgisrally.org; www.rallyinfo.com.

Cost: Not so much to quite a lot, depending on your bike, your tastes, your accommodations, and more. But the price tag doesn't have to be prohibitive. Figure about $100 a day to participate in the Mother Road Rally.

54 Bike It
Bicycle the Countryside of America or Europe

Feel the burn—in your calves and thighs, that is—as you see the world via pedal power. Take the trip in one long journey or string together occasional short rides over as long as you like. Try a coast-to-coast trek in North America or Europe or something much less daunting.

If grueling tests of stamina appeal to you but riding coast to coast doesn't, consider pedaling—or at least following the route of—Europe's famed Tour de France. Closer to home, the 405-mile Ride the Rockies offers scenery, camaraderie, and a hilly workout through the Colorado Rockies every summer.

Left: A motorcycle trek could be just the ticket to new freedom and new friends.
Above right: Bicycle your way across the country.

The less ambitious cyclist might try coasting through California's wine country, cruising Hawaii's Big Island, or sightseeing around Chicago. Across the Atlantic, a moderate ride rich in cultural history and scenery is along Austria's scenic Danube.

UltimatePedal:

Try a ride for charity.

Reality Check:

This is not for the out-of-shape biker.

What It Takes to Get There:

50plus Expeditions, www.50plusexpeditions.com; Euro-Bike & Walking Tours, www.eurobike.com; Ride the Rockies, www.ridetherockies.com; Velo Echappé (Tour de France ride), www.veloechappe.com; Bicycle Adventures, www.bicycleadventures.com; www.viator.com.

Cost: Danube, eight days at about $1,400, with 50 Plus Expeditions; a week in Tuscany, $2,100 to $2,800 with Euro-Bike & Walking Tours; Ride the Rockies, $285 registration fee; the Tour de France, about $5,400 with Velo Echappé; Chicago, about $30.

55 Take a Hike
Follow the Appalachian Trail

Start with sturdy shoes. The trek along the eastern half of the United States covers more than 2,100 miles from Springer Mountain, Georgia, to Katahdin, Maine, over literally all types of terrain. Whether you're a NOBO (trail lingo for a northbound hiker) or a SOBO (southbound), go prepared and go for fun. Hike portions of the trail or take the time to journey the entire route.

Get ready to join a huge club of fellow hikers and trail aficionados, too. The trail is popular and its community passionate about the pursuit and protection of this unique piece of the American legend. Check out a few of the hikers' stories online.

UltimateHike:

Join one of the Appalachian Trail clubs along the East Coast, and enjoy one of their trips to restore and maintain the trail, or you can just pitch in during the summer as a volunteer.

Reality Check:

Don't be fooled. Even in North America's smaller mountains, trail conditions can change unexpectedly and become extremely harsh. Go prepared. If you're serious about the trek, don't skimp on the hiking boots, either. It's a long way to walk, especially in uncomfortable or ill-fitting boots.

The Appalachian Trail Conservancy, www.appalachiantrail.org; Appalachian Long Distance Hikers Association, www.aldha.org; American Hiking Society, www.amerianhiking.org; "The Appalachian Trail Home Page" www.fred.net/kathy/at.html; Appalachian Trail Museum, www.atmuseum.org, www.n2backpacking.com; www.elderhostel.org.

Cost: Depends on your tastes, accommodations, and feet.

56 Climb It
Tackle Colorado's 14ers

Cody Downard/Vail Resorts

This is a Rocky Mountain high for real. Stand atop the world surrounded by the majesty of Colorado's mountains set against the cloudless blue sky. It's a spiritual experience tough to surpass, whether you're an outdoor enthusiast or not.

The Colorado Rockies boast 54 peaks that soar above 14,000 feet. They carry names like Quandary, Massive, Princeton, and Holy Cross.

Try climbing most of them or just one. You can even drive almost to the top of Mount Evans, which is just west of Denver. But the drive isn't for the fainthearted.

UltimateClimb:
Summit as many as possible.

Reality Check:
This is altitude, and it begins at a mile high. That's 5,280 feet above sea level, so before you aim for the sky, get in high-altitude shape. Also, as of press time, hiking on several of the peaks is banned because access trails cross private land.

What It Takes to Get There:

Colorado Fourteeners Initiative, www.14ers.org; Leave No Trace Center for Outdoor Ethics, www.lnt.org; Outward Bound West, www.outwardboundwest.com.

Cost: Travel to and from Colorado, and then supplies and boots; supported expeditions, such as an Outward Bound climb, cost extra. A 22-day Colorado backpacking experience runs approximately $3,000.

57 Nature at its Best
Try Wilderness Camping

Get away from a landscape pockmarked by urban sprawl. Experience America's wilderness in its pristine state, often without trails, facilities, campsites, or signs of earlier visitors. The U.S. government has designated more than 675 protected areas as wilderness and monitors them to preserve their unspoiled nature. It's about hiking and camping with nature in mind.

Left: The Appalachian Trail has a cadre of supporters, protectors, and fans, including the Appalachian Trail Conservancy.
Above: Beaver Creek (Colorado) Hiking Center sponsors an array of summer hikes.

Don't be shy if you're not an experienced camper. All you need is a sense of adventure and assistance from one of many reputable and highly competent outdoor outfitters to make a wilderness trek the trip of a lifetime.

As you ford a rough river rapid or hike a rugged canyon, imagine yourself as the first person to explore this terrain.

UltimateCamp:
Saddle up your horse or load your raft to see America as it once was. Two choices: the giant Frank Church River of No Return Wilderness Area in Idaho or Sequoia/Kings Canyon in California's Sierra Nevada.

Reality Check:
The National Park Service takes wilderness designations seriously, so if you're not willing to erase all trace of your presence there, this kind of camping isn't for you. No flush toilets or electric hairdryers here, either.

What It Takes to Get There:

Start with the National Park Service's official Web site, www.nps.gov; information, maps, and more, www.trails.com and click on Trail Finder; www.pilotguides.com; www.wilderness.net.

Cost: For do-it-yourselfers, only the cost of your supplies and nominal park fees.

58 Surf's Up
Hang Ten or Just Watch

Beginning surfers can start off in calm waves at seaside resorts or along coastlines in safe waters. Lessons generally are available.

Seasoned, undisputed experts, on the other hand, may think about tackling the ocean's roiling fury off the north shore of the Hawaiian island of Oahu in winter. These are serious waves. If they seem a bit out of your class, go for spectator sport instead. Catch Van's Triple Crown of Surfing in November and December to see the best of the best compete for top honors.

UltimateWave:
For experts only, dare to catch the endless wave— Rapid No. 11 on the Zambezi River in Africa.

Reality Check:
Learning to surf is a challenge that almost anyone with decent balance and in good shape can meet. On the other hand, tackling some of Earth's

mightiest waves should be reserved for the most expert daredevils.

What It Takes to Get There:

Hawaii Visitors and Convention Bureau, www.gohawaii.com; travel agent sites, including www.greathawaiivacations.com; The Surfer's Directory, www.boardfolio.com; www.triplecrownofsurfing.com; Hans Hedemann Surf School, www.hhsurf.com; www.isurfing.com; www.surfline.com.

Cost: Varies depending on where you go; travel packages can cut the fare or save your frequent-flier miles; surfing lessons in Hawaii, one-hour group lesson from about $50 (Hans Hedemann Surf School).

59 Scuba the World's Waters
Explore Earth's Other 70 Percent

Dive the deep holes of North America's freshwater springs. Meander the great living coral reefs of the Pacific, or cruise the waters of the Turks and Caicos in the British West Indies. Water dominates the Earth, so your choices and options are endless. Spin the globe and find your starting point.

If you're not an experienced diver, no problem. Lessons are available almost everywhere. Make sure you choose a reputable organization, then get started, get certified, and get ready to descend to another world.

UltimateDive:

It depends on your tastes. Abundant coral reefs create a sea-life mecca in Micronesia, especially Truk. Florida features intense deep holes for cave divers, or you might try skin diving and spearfishing off Mexico's Baja Peninsula.

Reality Check:

Not everyone takes to underwater diving. If it's not your thing, try snorkeling. It's closer to the surface, requires almost no training, and underwater views can be spectacular. It's also a great way to pass the time if a spouse prefers the deep waters below.

What It Takes to Get There:

Start with www.thescubaguide.com for scuba basics, instructor information, trips, and gear reviews. For lessons, check with local dive shops and then get references; www.diversdirect.com for equipment price comparisons; www.asiatranspacific.com.

Cost: The bare gear essentials easily can top $500; an alternative—try the relatively low-cost option of a basic scuba class at a resort, rental gear included; several lessons for less than $100; snorkel equipment rental for generally a few dollars a day.

60 Mush with the Pack
Learn to Dogsled

Imagine just you and your team of dogs slicing across the frozen tundra, straining against the icy wind. It's not the Iditarod or a scene from *Snow Dogs*. The adrenaline flows all the same.

Top left: It's not the wilderness, but the scenery is as beautiful on a horseback ride at Spear-o-Wigwam Ranch in Wyoming. Left: Surfing is ageless for the experts. Above: Get ready to see new worlds underwater.

Head to the mountains and learn what it takes to command a team of supreme canine athletes. You'll learn how to care for the animals, pick up new lingo, and then take control. You may find yourself joining a mushing club.

UltimateSled:

Alaska's Iditarod.

Reality Check:

No expertise needed, but mushing does require relatively good physical fitness, balance, and agility. If you're not up to the physical requirements, try sled-dog rides instead. Plenty of outfitters and even ski resorts offer them regularly.

What It Takes to Get There:

For links to organizations worldwide, www.sleddogcentral.com; www.ne-outfitters.com; www.selectalaska.com; www.alaskadogsledding.com; www.iditarod.com; www.ooowoo.com.
Check with individual ski resorts, including www.vailresorts.com, for sled-dog outfitters.

Cost: Alaska mushing, approximately $250 for a half-day lesson and about $3,000 for long tours; in the lower 48, $25 and up for lessons or rides.

61 Extreme Competition
Train For and Finish a Marathon or Triathlon

Ever wonder if you have what it takes? If your body is in good shape, the patience and discipline of age may be just your ticket to success. Plenty of your peers regularly run marathons and complete triathlons. Physical fitness aside, youngsters often lack the mental stamina to tackle the grueling training and endure mile after mile of pounding pavement and burning muscle required to cross the finish line.

If a full marathon seems too imposing, set a goal of completing a half-marathon and go from there. Who knows? You could exceed your wildest dreams.

UltimateEndurance:

Qualify for and then finish Hawaii's Ironman Triathlon. Join 1,800 participants ages 18 to 80 as they shoot for a 2.4-mile ocean swim, 112-mile bike race, and 26.2-mile run in a maximum 17 hours. Qualifying races are worldwide.

Ken Redding/Vail Resorts

Reality Check:

Because you're older, training is a full-time pursuit that doesn't happen overnight. You're not a kid anymore, so don't expect miracles. On the other hand, don't give up before you get started.

What It Takes to Get There:

Runner's World, www.runnersworld.com; www.ironmanlive.com, the official site of the Ironman® Triathlon; www.halhigdon.com; www.popularfitness.com.

Cost: Spring for good running shoes (about $100), fill up your water bottle (often free) or pack, and head out the door. Check local running stores and organizations for race registration costs.

Oar Revoir
Kayak the World's Rivers, Lakes, and Oceans

Slide by ice shelves in Antarctica. Cruise with orcas off Alaska. Challenge the whitewater of a mountain-fed stream. Or simply glide the glass surface of a local lake. Kayaking is a personal sport that can be as exhilarating or as mellow as you choose. Boats come big and small, fit for one or two, and can be inflatable—a ducky—or hard-shell.

Choose your water depending on your skill and stamina. All levels of kayak schools and classes—some even at the local swimming pool—are designed to fit your needs. Mix kayaking with a raft trip and take along some family members for a multigenerational experience.

Left: Try a dogsled ride near Vail, Colorado, or learn to drive your own team. Top left: Get ready to test your endurance with a marathon run. Above: A kayak glides across Lake Tahoe.

UltimateRapids:

Kayak wild waters by day and camp under the stars by night.

Reality Check:

Arm strength is required, as is the ability to briefly hang upside down if you roll the kayak. If dizziness is an issue, try a ducky. It dumps you out instead of rolling over.

What It Takes to Get There:

American Canoe Association, www.acanet.org; www.paddlesports.com; www.outsidehiltonhead.com; www.paddlermagazine.com also has an international searchable database; www.raftidaho.com; www.freshairadventure.com.

Cost: $400 and up for the kayak, plus your gear. Consider taking lessons and/or a guided tour (gear included) instead; less than $100 for half-day barrier island excursion, about $300 for a three-day ride, all equipment included, Hilton Head Island, South Carolina; $1,800 for a six-day trip on Idaho's Main Salmon River, lodge stays. Beginning lessons and senior clinics as low as $40 (New Brunswick, Canada's Bay of Fundy).

63 Out of this World
Train Like an Astronaut

Heavenly dreams become simulated reality at Aviation Challenge® or Space Academy® in Huntsville, Alabama, or the Astronaut Training Experience (ATX) at Kennedy Space Center, Florida.

Most people at least once have wondered what it would be like to see Earth from the heavens; float in zero gravity; or withstand the 4G force of

a space launch. The more ambitious have dreamed of piloting a mission to space or joining a shuttle crew.

Space Academy® is a safe and comfortable way to do just that. Feel as if you're walking on the moon in a gravity trainer; tumble in space in the multi-axis trainer; scuba dive in an underwater astronaut trainer and proceed through the check-list with "Mission Control."

UltimateSpace:

Get your shot of actual reality with Space Adventures, Arlington, Virginia, which operates commercial orbital spaceflights and training. In partnership with the Russians, it even has sent a civilian to the International Space Station. If price is no object, sign up and start training today.

Reality Check:

Simulators and training are as close as most of us will ever get to space travel. What a great and fun way to experience the last frontier.

What It Takes to Get There:

Space Camp® Online, www.spacecamp.com; Space Adventures, www.spaceadventures.com.

Cost: Space Academy® and Aviation Challenge® from $400 for a weekend to $3,000 for eight days; Space Adventures from $1,000 for Spaceflight Club membership to $20 million for a roundtrip ride and one week at the space station.

Head in the Clouds
Try Hot-Air Ballooning

If you're not ready for a trip to space and can't quite afford to ante up a cool $20 million, perhaps you might want to go sky-high in a hot-air balloon. It's a definite step up from a down-to-earth experience.

In case you haven't looked up lately, plenty of people are taking to the skies in brilliantly colored balloons of all shapes and sizes. Float with the wind and experience the sensation of the Earth revolving beneath you. The Montgolfier brothers definitely had the right idea.

An added bonus is that you'll meet great people and have the opportunity to travel nationwide to various balloon festivals.

If you don't want to pilot a balloon, consider crewing for someone else. It's a heady experience and usually comes with the perk of free flights.

UltimateRide:

Participate in the world-famous Albuquerque, New Mexico, balloon festival.

Reality Check:

Take lessons, take your time, and have a blast. Also be aware of rules and regulations associated with ballooning in a specific area.

What It Takes to Get There:

www.cdli.ca/CITE/balloon.htm; www.eballoon.org; Balloon Federation of America, www.bfa.net; Sportal of North American Balloon Association, www.eballoon.com; www.hotairballoon.org; www.hot-air-ballooning.org.

Cost: Take a ride in the sky for about $160 and up per person.

Top left: Space Adventures Ltd. helped Dorothy Simpson, 80, enjoy a zero-gravity flight in 2004 aboard a Russian Ilyushin-76. Above right: Bright balloons fill fields and sky at a New Mexico festival.

Reality Check:

These vehicles are not toys. With high-powered supercars the adrenaline rush is high but so is the demand for skill. Take driving seriously, follow your fantasy, and have a blast.

What It Takes to Get There:

www.racingschools.com links to all kinds of racing schools, even Kart racing; Mario Andretti Racing School, www.andrettiracing.com; Jeff Gordon Racing School, www.jeffgordonracingschool.com; Dale Jarrett Racing Adventure, www.racingadventure.com; SpeedTech Auto Racing Schools, www.tospeed.com.

Cost: About $75 to $150 to ride as a passenger and up to $3,500 for training and 130 laps or so around Talladega International in Alabama; up to $15,000 to race with a pro; $800 for 14 laps in an Indy car at Texas Motor Speedway.

65 Start Your Engine
Drive a Race Car

Put the pedal to the metal literally and learn to do it the right way from the best by taking a class at one of the world's many driving schools. Get behind the wheel of all models of cars—Indy, NASCAR, Formula, dragster, Kart, rally, sport racers, off-road, and even your own.

Test your stock-car stamina against professionals. Take a few laps around Talladega. Slip into the controlled power of an Indy car or explosive thrust of a dragster. Become an expert performance driver in your street car. Many of the greatest legends in motor sports lend their names, expertise, and reputations to driving schools worldwide.

UltimateDrive:
Race a champion.

66 Powder Power
Ski the Great Resorts of the World

From Vail, Colorado, to Innsbruck, Austria, and Big Sky, Montana, to St. Moritz, Switzerland, the snow-covered slopes beckon skiers, boarders, and spectators of all shapes and skill levels. Throw in the excitement of travel to these legendary high spots, and even the not-so-fervent skier pays

Jack Affleck/Vail Resorts

Top: Try an Indy car at Mario Andretti Racing School. Above: Enjoy a Rocky Mountain high at Vail, Colorado. Top right: Take in the towering views in Nepal with Geographic Expeditions.

attention. Any way you cut it, skiing makes winter a lot more fun.

Picture yourself dangling in a gondola across the huge chasms of the Alps. Gaze at the majestic Pyrenees. See your breath through the drifting champagne powder of the Rockies.

Feel the cold against your cheeks? It's a perfect day in high-mountain paradise.

UltimateSki:
Try helicopter skiing in Canada. Cross-country skiing on less-crowded terrain is an alternative. Try the 10th Mountain Division Hut Association's hut-to-hut treks in the Rockies.

Reality Check:
Plan your trips over several years. The anticipation likely will be almost as heady as the powder itself. And you don't even have to ski. The people-watching at a ritzy resort is phenomenal. Don't overlook staying in lower-cost venues or buying used or closeout equipment.

What It Takes to Get There:
Try Web sites for individual resorts and regions; Over the Hill Gang International, www.othgi.com; http://europe.ski.com; www.skicountryusa.com; www.ski.com; Cross Country Ski Areas Association, www.xcski.org; www.snowlink.com; www.canadianheli-skiing.com; www.huts.org.

Cost: Downhill skiing and boarding are costly sports; lift tickets, around $50 a day and up; lodging often requires multinight stays; three-day Canadian heli-ski package about $4,000; seven nights to Sun Valley, Idaho, about $1,225 to $1,540 (Over the Hill Gang International).

67 Top of the World
Trek to Mount Everest Base Camp

Definitely a possibility on a climber's Adventures of a Lifetime to-do list is to stand before nature's ultimate peak, Mount Everest. At 29,035 feet high, its towering beauty will take your breath away—literally. The elevation of Base Camp, where most climbers begin their ascent of the mountain, is more than 17,550 feet.

Everest has been the stuff of climbing legend since long before its first conquerors, Sir Edmund Hillary and Tenzig Norgay, stood triumphant atop the summit in 1953.

And in case you think you're too old for the trek, in 2003 Yuichiro Miura, 70, became the oldest man to summit the peak.

UltimatePeak:
Being there!

Reality Check:
The faint of heart and the casual summer athlete have no place here. No matter how fit you think you are, think twice and train three times as hard before tackling this challenge.

Reputable outfitters and guides are a must, so do your homework. Some places to start include the online Himalayan trekking guidebook at www.YetiZone.com; www.mounteverest.net; www.geox.com from Geographic Expeditions; www.nepalvista.com; www.k2news.com; www.gapadventures.com; Kirat Treks Adventure Travel, www.kirattreks.com; www.realadventures.com. Good reading at www.rgs.org from the Royal Geographic Society.

Cost: About $2,000 and up, depending on length of trek, starting point, outfitter, and type of accommodations.

68 Experience a Free Fall
Learn to Parachute or Skydive

Crazy or courageous? That depends on how one approaches this gut-wrenching experience. Initial stomach jitters are virtually guaranteed the first time out the plane's door, but then so is the thrill of open-air free fall and the feel of exhilarating accomplishment after it's over. You're also likely to want to go right back up.

Parachuting and skydiving are among those thrilling endeavors that most people have dreamed of at one time or another. Remember

former President George H.W. Bush celebrating his 75th and also his 80th birthday with parachute jumps? You can jump, too, if you're up for it.

UltimateJump:

Try hang gliding for a particularly soaring sense of accomplishment.

Reality Check:

If you're not ready to go it alone, consider a tandem jump with an expert. That's how Bush did it on his 80th. Make sure your jump is planned through a competent group or organization. Check them out before you jump. Don't skimp on safety for the sake of price.

What It Takes to Get There:

United States Parachute Association, www.uspa.org; www.dropzone.com; your local Yellow Pages or business database under *parachuting, skydiving,* and *hang gliding.*

Cost: About $150 and up; pay the extra $50 and up to video or photograph your feat. It makes great fodder for "fish" stories.

69 Bank on an Adrenaline Rush
Try Whitewater Rafting

Leave civilization and your cell phone behind. Enjoy nature's tranquility and its fury as you experience whitewater rafting, unspoiled river beaches, and breathtaking mountain vistas by day and canopies of stars by night. No experience—or effort—required.

Whether rafting Africa's mighty Zambezi, China's raging Yangtze, or Idaho's pristine Main Salmon, the adrenaline rush and adventure are unmatched for sports enthusiasts and armchair dreamers alike.

Rafting and outdoor options are available for all levels of skill and adventurousness. Options often include lodging and other accommodations as well as paddle, guided-oar, and motorized rafts and boats, depending on the river.

UltimateWhitewater:

Consider a 17-day trip through the Grand Canyon or run a river via ducky, a rubber kayak. The latter takes strength and stamina with thrills guaranteed. Outside the United States, try a trip on Tibet's Upper Yangtze.

For the wildest ride, plan a trip when a river's volume is at its peak—often in late spring—then brace yourself for some serious whitewater!

Reality Check:

Be honest about your skill level. A life (including yours) could depend on it. Intrigued by the idea, but not sure a long rafting trip is for you? Try a half- or full-day trip on a nearby river first.

What It Takes to Get There:

For international whitewater outfitters, check out www.gordonsguide.com, www.earthriver.com, or www.americanoutdoors.org. Closer to home, for outfitters on the Main Salmon, check out www.raftidaho.com; www.gonorthwest.com, click on Idaho, then whitewater rafting; for Grand Canyon outfitters, go to www.nps.gov/grca/river/river_concessioners.htm.

Cost: Weeklong trips in the United States, about $1,200 and up; senior discounts often available. International trips, a 19-day trip on the Upper Yangtze about $5,000.

70 One for the Books
Make the *Guinness Book of World Records*

For people who aspire to fame—even if it's fleeting—attempting to set a world record can be an excellent pastime. It also can test your creative genius. After all, how often does someone immediately associate carving chain links in a toothpick with setting a world record?

Left: Former President George Bush parachuted to celebrate his 75th birthday. He did it again on his 80th.
Above: Rafters thrill to the whitewater on the Rouge River in Quebec, Canada.

If you're game to go for a record, try it alone or with friends and keep in mind that getting there may be half the fun. In fact, it could be the most fun you'll ever have for free.

Some sample records set by seniors:

- Senator John Glenn: Oldest male astronaut at age 77 and 103 days when he went up in the U.S. space shuttle *Discovery,* October, 29, 1998.

- George Blair, Winter Garden, Florida, oldest water skier at age 87 and 18 days in Winter Garden, Florida, February 10, 2002.

- Otto Comanos, Australia, oldest windsurfer when he retired at age 89 in 1986.

- Flossie Bennett, 97, United Kingdom, oldest bridesmaid since 1999.

UltimateRecord:
The one you set.

Reality Check:
The officials at the Guinness Book have specific procedures and rules that must be followed. Check its Web site for specifics and don't forget to have witnesses and take pictures of your record-setting feat.

What It Takes to Get There:
The official site of the Guinness Book is www.guinnessworldrecords.com.

Cost: Your time, any supplies, and of course the price of the book ($18.75 at www.amazon.com) to marvel at your accomplishment.

71 Links to the Past
Play Golf at St. Andrews

Visit the birthplace of golf, the links at Scotland's St. Andrews, where golf has been played since around 1457.

Walk the paths of golf's legends, past and present. Many a British Open has been played at St. Andrews, and you can almost imagine Ben Hogan, Jack Nicklaus, or Tiger Woods stepping off the tee box at No. 9 on the Old Course. Let your imagination run wild: Hoist aloft the venerable Open's silver "Claret Jug" trophy, your reward for a day's play in the fabled Scottish breeze or whipping wind!

UltimateGolf:
Stay at St. Andrews Old Course Hotel and play all six St. Andrews courses. For the more ambitious, go beyond the St. Andrews experience and play as many of the world's great courses as possible, and then try to make the cut for the PGA Seniors Tour.

Reality Check:

Above: Senator John Glenn holds the record as the oldest male astronaut. Top right: A shot of the venerable St. Andrews. Right: Cast your line at Rainbow Trout Ranch, Colorado.

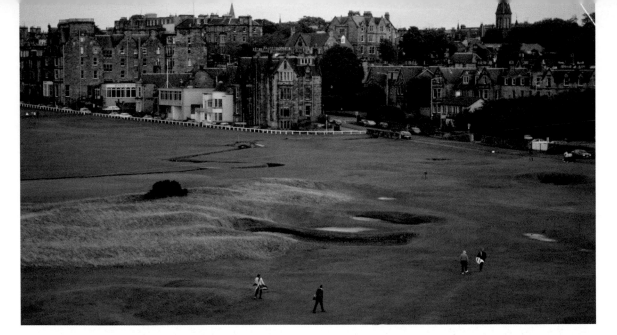

St. Andrews offers more than birdies and bogies. Don't miss The Royal and Ancient Golf Clubhouse and the British Golf Museum at St. Andrews.

What It Takes to Get There:

www.standrews.com; www.opengolf.com; www.pga.com; www.europeantour.com; www.standrews.org.uk.

Cost: Equipment as well as greens and other fees easily can top $200 to $500 a day, depending on the course.

Hook, Line, and Sinker
Fish the Great Rivers, Lakes, and Oceans

Fishing is a passion for some, a sport for others, and a pleasure to anyone who happens upon this opportunity to relax outdoors.

The options are limitless. Cast your line into cascading Frying Pan in Colorado on the quest to outsmart a brook or brown trout; or steel yourself in anticipation of the jaw-jarring bite of a giant peacock bass in Brazil's Pousada Rio Roosevelt. Take a king salmon on the Kenai in Alaska. Some liken the fishing for rainbows around Kamchatka, Russia, to that of Alaska years ago. Try saltwater challenges in the waters off Costa Rica or cast a line off almost any pier and try your luck. Go on a day or night adventure or simply while away a few hours. It's up to you.

UltimateCast:
Hook the big one.

Reality Check:
Wherever you fish, pay attention to local fishing laws and ordinances.

What It Takes to Get There:

http://saltfishing.about.com; www.pierfishing.com; www.adventuresports.com and click on Fishing/Hunting for lots of links; www.fishquest.com lists trips, international and domestic, by species; www.peacockbassfishing.com; www.cabelas.com.

Cost: Fishing license, about $10 to $40, depending on the state; senior discounts may apply.

Experience It Live

73 Run for the Roses
Experience the Kentucky Derby

Whether you're a horse enthusiast or a fan of spirit, pomp, and tradition, head to Louisville, Kentucky, for the Kentucky Derby. The first jewel of racing's Triple Crown is the ultimate race and a symbol of what Thoroughbred racing is all about.

The world's finest three-year-old equine athletes take to the 1¼-mile track at Churchill Downs on the first Saturday of every May in their quest for the roses. The winner receives a blanket of red roses. Other Derby traditions call for magnificent and immaculately groomed horses, their jockeys in brightly colored silks, and elegantly dressed women in spectacular hats squired by well-dressed men. Sipping mint juleps trackside is practically de rigueur.

UltimateHorseRace:
Go for the Triple Crown. See the Derby, Preakness Stakes at Pimlico in Baltimore, and Belmont Stakes in Elmont, New York.

Reality Check:
Don't assume you can get a ticket to the Derby. They're tough to come by, at least at a reasonable price. Application to buy tickets directly from Churchill Downs needs to be made well ahead of time. Of course, you can pay top dollar from ticket resellers online or ante up big bucks and enter your own winning Thoroughbred in the Run for the Roses.

What It Takes to Get There:
www.churchilldowns.com; www.gotoLouisville.com.

Cost: General admission, $40; reserved seating about $300 and up from resellers; $100 and up for Preakness and Belmont.

74 A Hostel World
Take a Different Travel Route

Traveling around the world or across the country needn't be expensive or limited to touring cathedrals or visiting historic places.

The nonprofit Elderhostel offers unique, memorable, and educational adventures for those 55 or older interested in seeing and learning about the world—and that includes your own backyard.

Try going solo, with a partner, or in a large group. Take long trips or short getaways. Elderhostel offers camaraderie, convenience, and education in a comfortable and secure environment.

Instead of just seeing the Grand Canyon, bike its rim and learn about its archaeology, and then raft the Colorado River deep below. Discover the ancient traditions of Japan and learn how the country has assimilated foreign influences into its unique culture. Board a rail car that's your moving classroom through Mexico's remote Barrancas del Cobre, or Copper Canyon.

The nonprofit Elderhostel also offers "Road Scholar" trips that are billed as more "experiential." Additionally, it funds the Lifelong Learning Institutes Network, an association of independent programs at institutes of higher learning across North America.

UltimateTrip:
There are so many adventures, it's hard to choose just one.

Reality Check:
Trip accommodations vary.

What It Takes to Get There:
www.elderhostel.org; www.bootsnall.com; www.tripadvisor.com for hostel reviews.

Cost: Varies; 16 days to Japan, about $4,700; 5 nights in Chicago, $800 to $1,000; Copper Canyon by train, 7 nights, about $1,700; 12 nights to Egypt, about $3,000.

75 Gotham at Its Best
Christmas in New York

Share the incredible energy that pulses through this First City of America. Enjoy the spirit, catch a show, take the ferry to the Statue of Liberty, wander the halls of Ellis Island, pause for a tribute at Ground Zero, admire the towering Christmas tree at Rockefeller Center and then take to the ice, tease your palate with some of the world's finest cuisine, shop, museum-hop, and, of course, thrive on the city's energy. Don't miss the view from Rockefeller Center's newly reopened observation deck, either. It's spectacular.

UltimateApple:
Times Square on New Year's Eve. Join the energized masses that flood Times Square as the giant illuminated ball descends the flagpole atop One

Above left: Thoroughbreds thunder down the track at Churchill Downs in Louisville, Kentucky. Above: A participant in Elderhostel's Active Outdoor program enjoys the view in Death Valley.

Times Square. It could be the largest and most fun party you'll ever attend. Come early, stay late, and don't worry about out-of-control mobs. That's not the norm here. Young and old come to enjoy an American tradition that's taken place almost every year since 1904.

Reality Check:
It's a big, bustling, multicultural city that's not for the timid.

What It Takes to Get There:

Some good starting places: www.NYC.gov and click on Visitors from the menu at left that leads to myriad links, or www.NewYork.com.

Cost: New York is the most expensive city in North America and among the most expensive in the world. A regular hotel room easily costs several hundred dollars a night. Suites at luxury hotels in Manhattan cost in the four figures.

76 National Treasure
Explore Washington, D.C.

Even in an era marred by terrorism and security concerns, the U.S. capital offers visitors a unique opportunity to see America's nerve center up close and to experience democracy at work.

The pride and patriotism inspired by standing in front of the White House or at the Tomb of the Unknowns in Arlington National Cemetery are inescapable. From the stark reminder of the Vietnam Memorial to the brilliance of a performance at the Kennedy Center for the Performing Arts, the nation's capital will move your heart and soul.

Visit the Library of Congress, the largest library in the world. Marvel at the architecture and then tour the U.S. Capitol, a world-recognized symbol of democracy. Tour the Senate, House, or White House. Gaze at a thoughtful Albert Einstein,

Above: Cartier's on Fifth Avenue in New York is decked out for Christmas. Top right: The Capitol in Washington, D.C., is a symbol of democracy. Right: The Bellagio lights up the Las Vegas night.

imposing Abraham Lincoln, or venerable George Washington, all captured in bronze as monuments to their accomplishments.

UltimatePatriot:

Spend a day as a spectator in Congress. Contact your congressman or congresswoman for information and access.

Reality Check:

Be prepared to face plenty of security checkpoints and a visible security-force presence. Lines to get tickets required for tours or to visit monuments and buildings may be long, with distribution on a first-come, first-served basis beginning at 9 AM. Summer is usually the busiest time.

What It Takes to Get There:

The Architect of the Capitol, www.aoc.gov; www.house.gov; www.loc.gov; www.senate.gov; www.whitehouse.gov, then follow the links to History & Tour information.

Cost: Tours and monuments often free, but tickets required for access.

Viva Las Vegas
Stars and Strip Light Up the Desert

Gamblers, food fanatics, fun fans, dance lovers, rockers, racers, shoppers, and dreamers all can get lucky in Las Vegas. Along with the megahotels sprouting from the desert, Sin City has grown up. It's a multicultural, international vacation mecca.

Watch Celine Dion or Andrea Boccelli perform; dance all night in a disco; eat an incredible, romantic meal against the backdrop of Bellagio's dancing fountains; stand atop the Paris Las Vegas half-size replica of the Eiffel Tower; dare to ride the Stratosphere's roller coaster 1,000 feet above the ground; take a helicopter tour of the Grand Canyon; descend inside towering nearby Hoover Dam; shop the discount outlets or haute couture; and, of course, gamble anywhere and everywhere.

Above all, don't write off Las Vegas as only a place to gamble. Its sights, sounds, and energy are worth experiencing at least once even if you never place a single bet.

UltimateOasis:

Las Vegas is over the top and proud of it. Excess is the norm, and luxury is no exception. Stay at one of the city's top hotels like the spectacular Bellagio or Wynn and be truly pampered.

Reality Check:

Smoking and gambling go hand in hand. If you don't smoke and don't like being in the midst of it, insist on a nonsmoking room at your hotel.

What It Takes to Get There:

www.lasvegas.com; www.lvchamber.com; www.visitlasvegas.com; www.bellagio.com; www.wynnlasvegas.com.

Cost: Check with your travel agent for deals.

78 Three, Two, One, Ignition . . .
Watch a Space Launch

Space exploration has journeyed far since the days of the Soviet *Sputniks* and America's *Echo I* and *II*. Satellites stud the sky. Man has walked on the moon. *Voyager* is on Mars. A space station orbits the Earth. It's nonetheless electrifying to stand at Cape Canaveral, Florida, and feel the energy as rocket engines ignite, then lift off in an explosion of flame and power heading to space.

A trip to Cape Canaveral for a launch means participating in and understanding the evolution of space exploration in your lifetime. It makes the dream a reality. Remember the days when people dressed up to fly on airplanes and no one had a computer? Someday space flight will be taken for granted, too.

UltimateBlastoff:

Watch a rocket launch from the Kennedy Space Center; try Kennedy's ATX, a daylong interactive Astronaut Training Experience.

Reality Check:

Stake out your viewing site early.

What It Takes to Get There:

www.kennedyspacecenter.com; www.nasa.gov, then click on Kennedy Space Center link; city of Cape Canaveral, http://fcn.state.fl.us/cape.

Cost: ATX, $225/person; admission and tours, $17 and up; lunch with an astronaut, $20.

Catch the Checkered Flag

Fans' Hearts Race at Fabled Tracks

For race fans, the words Daytona, Talladega, Darlington, and Indy represent not towns but the pinnacle of auto racing. These are the places where men (and women) and machines battle bumper to bumper, nose to tail, at mesmerizing speeds for the checkered flags and the right to be called champions.

For a spectator, the experience consists of you, about a quarter-million other people, and unbelievable surround sound that makes you vibrate from head to toe. Try one race or turn into a NASCAR or Indy groupie and follow the circuit. You'll meet tons of people, visit fun places, and become part of a favorite, and growing, American pastime.

If you can't make race day, tracks usually offer guided tours. Daytona in a van at 70 mph isn't quite like watching Jimmie Johnson take a bank at speeds of more than 160 mph, but it does give a visitor newfound respect for the racers.

UltimateFan:

Snag a pit pass on race day. Some tracks allow you to buy them.

Reality Check:

NASCAR and Indy Racing are hot. Expect huge crowds and higher rates for lodging. Reserved-seat tickets can be difficult to get and, if you can find them, expensive to buy. Try searching for a travel package through individual speedways that may include race-day tickets.

What It Takes to Get There:

www.nascar.com;
www.daytonaintlspeedway.com;
www.talladegasuperspeedway.com;
www.indianapolismotorspeedway.com;
www.darlingtonraceway.com.

Cost: Daytona 500, $100 and up; Brickyard, $35 to $85; Indianapolis 500, $40 to $150; Talladega Superspeedway, $45 to $115. All prices are approximate, for single-day tickets.

Take Center Ice

Skate at Rockefeller Center

Most of us have grown up with the image from television, postcards, and movies: tall buildings framing the famed statue of Atlas with the world on his shoulders and the ice rink and giant Christmas tree in the background. This is New York City's Rockefeller Center in winter and your chance to live the postcard.

It may be only frozen water surrounded by restaurants and a shopping mall, but even the most mundane things in New York impart their own unique energy. Skate, then warm yourself while shopping at dozens of stores, catch the Rockettes

---

Left: The space shuttle *Atlantis* is rolled out at Kennedy Space Center in Florida. Above: Follow your dreams and watch the world's top race drivers compete at the top tracks.

at Radio City, and end the day with dinner overlooking the beautiful lights of the center and city. Not bad for a trip to the mall.

UltimateRockefeller:
Mix your skating with a weekend in New York for maximum enjoyment.

Reality Check:
It's not the best ice, but it certainly is the best view and place to see and be seen. This is the quintessential New York experience, so the rink can get crowded. Try going in the early morning or later in the day for fewer crowds.

What It Takes to Get There:

www.rockefellercenter.com;
http://gonyc.about.com and click on Attractions;
www.cyberrentals.com.

Cost: $7 to $12 for rink admission depending on days and dates; lessons, around $30.

81 Have a Ball

Attend a Game at Every Major League Stadium

Young or old, the vision is the same—sitting in the stands munching peanuts or popcorn, bellowing advice to the players on the field, leaping to your feet as the winning run scores. The great baseball stadiums—often red brick and black steel or iron—are steeped in history and share a treasured place in American lore.

The nation's MLB stadiums may not all look the same, but the experience of being in each one is yours to enjoy at 30 ballparks across the country; Yankee Stadium (New York) to Tropicana Field (Tampa Bay Devil Rays), Dodger Stadium (Los

Angeles) to Wrigley Field (Chicago Cubs), Minute Maid Park (Houston Astros) to Camden Yards (Baltimore Orioles).

Visit them all in one summer or over several seasons. The memories will be just as exciting, the pitches just as fast and furious.

UltimateBall:
Visit all the spring practice venues and take your favorite person with you.

Reality Check:
Hitting every park in one season is a major challenge. Perhaps consider spreading your trips out over a couple of seasons.

What It Takes to Get There:
www.ballparksofbaseball.com; www.mlb.com; also check individual team sites.

Cost: Travel is your choice; game tickets range from about $5 to $75 and up.

Can You Dig It?
Hunt for the Past

Brash Hollywood swashbuckler Indiana Jones, played by actor Harrison Ford, may have forever changed the world's image of an archaeologist. You can change it further by rolling up your sleeves and joining the quest for information about the past. An archaeological, anthropological, or geological dig is both a working and learning experience.

Left: Revel in the lights and life of New York City with a Christmastime whirl around Rockefeller Center's ice rink.
Above: Baseball is a uniquely American sport to watch, enjoy, and experience.

Dig down the street or across the world. Hunt for bits of history about the Earth, past peoples, flora, or fauna. Try it as a volunteer, spectator, or participant—all under expert supervision, of course.

Excavate shell middens (shells and other debris left by earlier inhabitants) on the coast of Maine; look for clues to the Wari, an ancient Andean civilization, in the mountains of Peru; or pursue hints to Neanderthal man in France.

UltimateDig:

Be party to a great find.

Reality Check:

Digging up the past may sound romantic, but the reality is that it's a long, slow, arduous process. Patient types only, please. It also involves bending over and digging. If that's too hard for you or digging in the dirt isn't appealing, consider a tour to visit sites in your area or somewhere across the world.

What It Takes to Get There:

The Arkansas Archaeological Society's list of Archaeological Parks in the U.S., www.uark.edu/misc/aras; more links to worldwide options, www.archaeolink.com; www.earthwatch.org; Archaeological Institute of America, www.archaeological.org then click on AIA Tours; www.gapadventures.com.

Cost: Ranges from free as a volunteer on a local dig to the sky's the limit for private jet tours of the world's sites; two weeks in Egypt, about $10,000.

83 Thar She Blows
Watch and Listen to the World's Whales

Make the connection with Earth's largest living mammal, the whale. It's a sight and an experience that chills and thrills.

Once you've seen these mighty Leviathans heave themselves out of the water in full breach and then plunge back headfirst, you're hooked for life, especially when you realize they're doing this all for fun.

You'll find yourself glued to the horizon for hours on end, listening for a labored hiss and looking for the spout of mist—signs that a whale has broken the surface to breathe. Watch humpback mothers and their newborn calves nuzzle beside you off Maui, great grays migrating off Oregon's Depoe Bay, blue whales in the Maldives, grays off Baja, sperm whales off New Zealand, and many more.

Why not wander the world to watch, listen to, and marvel at the whales.

UltimateExperience:
Snorkel the waters for a chance encounter.

Reality Check:
In most places, whales are protected by strict laws that can, on the surface, limit your encounters.

The trick—and luck—is to figure out where and when these magnificent creatures will surface next. You could end up closer than you expected.

What It Takes to Get There:
Whale-watching areas usually have many reputable charter and tour services; otherwise, www.whaleguide.com; Hawaiian Islands Humpback Whale National Marine Sanctuary, http://hawaiihumpbackwhale.noaa.gov.

Cost: Generally well under $100 per person for short trips; overnights, expeditions, and charters cost considerably more.

Left: Learning about the past from its fragments is painstaking work. Above: A killer whale is caught spyhopping—partially lifting its body out of the water—off Saturna Island, British Columbia, Canada.

84 Eye-to-Eye in the Wild
Go on Photo Safari in Africa

The king of beasts quietly contemplates the horizon. A cheetah is less patient, taking off in pursuit of a possible dinner. Herds of giraffe lumber across the savanna. Elsewhere, wildebeests, hippos, buffalo, baboons, elephants, flamingos, impalas, antelope, and cranes try to make a living.

Actually watching these amazing creatures go about their daily lives, seemingly oblivious to the enthralled visitors in a nearby truck, can seem surreal. Giant hippos float in pools to cool themselves. Giraffes munch leaves on tall trees. Herds of zebras graze the grasslands.

This isn't Tampa's Busch Gardens or the San Diego Zoo's Wild Animal Park in California. No tame beasts living in landscaped zoos, jumping, running, or nuzzling on cue. This is the real thing. Welcome to Africa's Serengeti, the Okavango Delta in the Kalahari Desert, Ngorongoro Crater, Lake Manyara, and other wildlife habitats.

Watch the animals by day from the safety of your vehicle, and then enjoy first-class lodge luxury or tented safari camping at night. Go for a few days or a few weeks.

UltimateSafari:
Try both the tent and lodge safaris and keep returning for a taste of the wild.

Reality Check:
Safari isn't cheap, but it's an amazing experience and well worth the expense. Consider going off season when rates are cheaper.

What It Takes to Get There:

Plenty of local African groups offer safaris. Always check references, however. Otherwise, Africa Travel Magazine, www.africa-ata.org; www.geoex.com; www.safarinow.com; www.africadreamsafaris.com; www.go2africa.com; www.e-gnu.com; www.leopard-tours.com.

Cost: A few hundred to a few thousand dollars and up, but the price usually includes a driver, accommodations, and food.

What It Takes to Get There:

The right attitude and recognition of local laws; American Association for Nude Recreation, www.aanr.com; www.nudist-resorts.org; http://gocalifornia.about.com, then click on Beaches or type "nudist" into search tool; www.nudeplaces.com; www.americannudist.com.

Cost: Free and up depending on location, property, and accommodations.

85 In the Buff
Visit a Nude or Clothing-Optional Venue

Remember the feeling of skinny-dipping as a kid in the backyard or at the lake? Free, unfettered, and natural—and perhaps frolicking in a secret spot or under cover of darkness.

Try it as an adult without your inhibitions at nude or clothing-optional camps, beaches, and resorts worldwide. The experience can be as natural to you as wearing clothes is to someone else.

Try a rustic woods experience, a private desert sojourn, or a luxurious beachside Caribbean vacation. Places like the secluded Black's Beach off San Diego or lesser-known spots like Odeceixe in Portugal offer nude or topless sunbathing. Resorts like Grand Lido Negril in Jamaica have clothing-optional pools and beaches.

UltimateBare:

Visit out of curiosity, stay for enjoyment.

Reality Check:

This isn't about sex; it's about shedding one's clothes as the natural thing to do, so don't expect everyone to be bathing beauties. Check any organization's references and reputation first. Also check for local nudity laws. First-timers should be extremely cautious of sunburn.

86 Ghostly Goings-On
Sleep in a Haunted Abode

The shadowy figure slowly ascends the stairs, then vanishes without a trace, and has done so for 125 years. Fact or fiction? You decide. Spend the night in a haunted castle, inn, or house for what could be a truly spine-tingling evening.

Do ghosts exist? Do restless spirits of murder victims wander aimlessly in a vain search for justice? Are the answers locked in the walls? You'll have to decide your answers for yourself. Solve the mystery and dispel the myths.

Left: Elephants share a familial moment in the wild. Above top: Perhaps a clothing-optional lifestyle appeals to you. Above right: Are you brave enough to spend the night in Castle Stuart's turreted East Tower?

You don't have to cross an ocean to find places that are reportedly haunted by specters. Some are undoubtedly closer than you think.

UltimateHaunt:

Spend time in several haunted spots, including the 17th century Castle Stuart near Inverness in the Scottish Highlands, and, of course, include a visit to The Witchery, reportedly Edinburgh's best and most haunted restaurant.

Reality Check:

Doesn't curiosity about reality draw you to the haunt in the first place?

What It Takes to Get There:

Local history associations and societies; www.adventurelandtravel.com, click on Unusual Lodging; www.whereintheworld.co.uk; www.castlestuart.com; a cyber portal to science, art and history, www.howardbloom.net; www.fabuloustravel.com, click on Weird Wanderings; www.thewitchery.com.

Cost: Varies dramatically depending on where you go.

87 Top/Bottom of the World
Stand Atop a Polar Cap

The privilege of standing on the frozen desolation at the top or bottom of the Earth is reserved for a select few people. Fortunately, with today's technology and transportation capability, you needn't have significant outdoor experience, be an expert skier, or trek hundreds of miles across frozen ice sheets to get to a polar cap.

The adventuresome in good physical shape can join expeditions that make the journey with the help of skis and snowmobiles, among other con-veyances. Others can opt for a more comfortable and quicker journey via helicopter to the geographic ends of the Earth.

What a not-so-tall-tale to tell your friends!

AlternativeAdventure:

Try an Antarctic cruise, or Greenland's Denmark Province, which is split by the Arctic Circle where the Atlantic and Arctic oceans meet.

Reality Check:

It's a long trek to the top or bottom of the Earth however you opt to get there. By helicopter north can take several days, and south ten days, including the air travel time to reach the helicopter embarkation points. Antarctic cruises can last several weeks or more.

Experience may not be required, but flexibility and the ability to adapt to unforeseen circumstances are. No tour operator has control over nature, but nature does affect transportation and weather.

Above: For a special polar experience consider booking passage on a Geographic Expedition North Pole trip via Russian icebreaker. Above right: Savor Norway's special beauty.

88

What It Takes to Get There:

Geographic Expeditions, www.geoex.com;
G.A.P Adventures, www.gapadventures.com;
www.adventuretrips.com; www.polartravel.co.uk;
http://away.com; www.quarkexpeditions.com;
www.allthevacations.com, then search under
Antarctica Expeditions or Arctic Expeditions.

Cost: About $2,000 and up; Geographic
Expedition's 16-day North Pole icebreaker trip,
about $19,000 and up; Quark's 26-day ship
experience, up to around $30,000.

In the Wake of Vikings
Sail the Fjords of Norway

Think of intense blue skies, dark glistening waters,
and the rosy color of the midnight sun. Combine
it with unparalleled natural beauty and Old World
charm for a taste of Norway, the northernmost
country of Scandinavia.

Journey through these natural wonders in big
ships on multiday destination cruises or try
smaller craft for short jaunts out of local towns
and villages.

Enjoy the people, the places, and the history of
this land of the Vikings.

UltimateSideTrip:

Take a Zodiac ride on Norway's maelstroms. These
are tremendously powerful whirlpools that churn
the bitter cold seas in the Lofoten Islands above
the Arctic Circle. It's definitely a powerful experience. Throughout history, the maelstroms have
sucked in many a sailor.

Reality Check:

Remember that Norway is north so that even in
the summer it can get chilly, especially at night.

What It Takes to Get There:

www.norway.com; www.fjords.com;
www.cruisenorway.com; www.fjordtravel.no;
www.fjord-pass.com.

Cost: 11-day trip, about $3,100 to $4,200; for do-it-yourselfers looking for day trips, pick up a fjord pass for hotel discounts.

89 Reef Beyond Belief
Marvel at Australia's Great Barrier Reef

Maybe it's the sound of the waves as they roll over offshore, the wet salt air that envelops you, or the pristine brilliance of the water. Maybe it's the idea of actually seeing the legendary Great Barrier Reef off Australia's northeastern coast. Although thousands of visitors from all over the world flock to this wonder every year, its tourist-attraction status fails to cloud the majesty of the world's largest natural coral reef.

Off the coast of Queensland, the unspoiled reef stretches more than 1,426 miles and is home to thousands of aquatic plants and animals.

Try viewing the reef from the sky. Take a helicopter or seaplane tour and marvel at its serpentine beauty. Or get up close and personal by snorkeling, diving, or just boating around it.

UltimateReef:

Charter a private yacht for a several-day trip for the best way to experience this natural wonder of the seas.

Reality Check:

The reef is a huge tourist attraction, so expect crowds. Alternatively, try the beautiful beaches elsewhere along Australia's coast. The reef and

environs are protected habitats with strict rules and regulations, so check with the Great Barrier Reef Marine Park Authority or other local organizations before fishing anywhere. If you check online for rates, many are in Australian dollars (convert them to U.S. dollars at www.xe.com).

What It Takes to Get There:

www.gbrmpa.gov.au from the
Great Barrier Reef Marine Park Authority;
www.barrierreefaustralia.com;
www.cultureandrecreation.gov.au;
www.greatbarrierreef.aus.net.

Cost: Sample day trips about $65 to $85, multiday trips, $375 and up.

Spiritual

Make a Pilgrimage
Visit a Place Sacred to Your Faith

Whatever your religion, a visit to one of its holy or sacred places can lead to a spiritual renewal or awakening. Somewhere with personal significance—a church, mosque, or synagogue of your childhood or the cemetery where a parent or loved one is buried—may also fan the flames of your faith.

The journey may lead to Jerusalem, Rome, or New Delhi; to Dublin, Ireland, or Dublin, Ohio. Muslims may make the hajj pilgrimage to Mecca in Saudi Arabia. Those of the Jewish faith may want to stand at the Wailing Wall in Jerusalem to fulfill a lifelong dream. Catholics may visit the Vatican and seek an audience with the Pope. In the spirit of true harmony and religious tolerance, you may even choose to visit a shrine or sacred place of a faith other than your own.

If you don't want to leave the country, look into Elderhostel's religious heritage programs.

UltimateFaith:
True spiritual peace.

Reality Check:
Before planning a trip abroad, check with the U.S. State Department to determine if travel to the area is allowed and is considered safe.

What It Takes to Get There:
Check with local religious groups; alternatively, www.tripadvisor.com; www.elderhostel.org; www.unitours.com; www.yahoo.com, follow links to religious travel; www.whereintheworld.co.uk, then click on Site Search.

Cost: Airfare from New York to Jerusalem (Tel Aviv), about $1,500 and up; airfare New York to New Delhi, about $2,600 and up; airfare New York to Rome, about $850. Cheaper fare specials generally available. Elderhostel program, five nights, about $530.

Top left: Australia's Great Barrier Reef snakes offshore for more than 1,400 miles. Above: The Wailing Wall in Jerusalem is perhaps the holiest site in Judaism.

91 A Broad Perspective

Learn About the World's Great Religions

Travel and learn more about the people and cultures of the world through their religions. Design your travels around the holy sites, major places of worship, libraries of teachings, or headquarters of some of the world's great religions.

Visit the gilded splendor of the Vatican in Rome. Walk in Jerusalem and stand among the holy places of Judaism, Islam, and Christianity. Experience India to feel the influence of Hinduism. Non-Muslims are strictly forbidden from the holiest city of Islam, Mecca, but may visit nearby Jeddah, a port on the Red Sea, to learn about the culture. Trying to sneak into Mecca isn't advisable. You risk execution.

The places to visit vary as much as the many religious beliefs of mankind. Enjoy your quest to better understand a few of them.

UltimateHarmony:
Learn something new and further world peace in the process.

Reality Check:
Be aware that war and unrest in the Middle East create many hazards for tourists. If you don't want to or can't make the trip, try a five-day Elderhostel program closer to home, "The World's Great Religions," in Hillsdale, Michigan. Similar programs are available elsewhere.

What It Takes to Get There:

www.tripadvisor.com; www.world66.com; www.hillmanwonders.com; www.elderhostel.org; www.religioustolerance.org.

Cost: Depends on your trip; airfare from New York to Jerusalem (Tel Aviv), about $1,500 and up; airfare New York to New Delhi, about $2,600 and up; Elderhostel program, about $530.

Indulgence

Gastronomic Delight
Enjoy the Finest Meal in the World

For the true connoisseur of fine food, the perfect meal is a sojourn in Nirvana.

Will the meal be a fusion of international flavors or those of one locale? Will the table be set in New York, Paris, Hong Kong, or somewhere off the beaten path? Will the sommelier bring out the finest French wines or rely on California or other vineyards? Will you opt for cognac or port? Which sauce? What garni? Beef, fish, veal, pork, chicken, or vegetarian? What about dessert? Is price an issue? What ambiance?

These consuming questions all require careful answers to carry out this indulgence to the fullest. After all, the finest meal in the world is in the palate of the beholder.

UltimateIndulgence:
Could it be that the world's best meal is in your own home with loved ones beside you?

Reality Check:
Finding where to go truly is a tough choice. Before you grab the nearest best-of-the-best list from a magazine or guidebook, keep in mind that your tastes may be very different from those of your companions.

What It Takes to Get There:
www.50bestrestaurants.co.uk;
www.foodandwine.com; www.thisisthelife.com;
www.viamichelin.com.

Cost: It's not a consideration. This is about an over-the-top experience.

Left: Sagaing in the Mandalay region of Myanmar (formerly Burma) boasts many excellent statues of Buddha.
Above: Anticipation could be one of the best parts of a quest for the ultimate meal.

93 The Pampered Guest
Spend the Night in Uncompromising Luxury

Stay at one of the great hotels or resorts of the world. Better yet, stay at several and then make up your own top-ten list. Let someone else cater to your comforts and needs and clean up after you. No bed-making or laundry days here!

Travel organizations and publications constantly come out with the latest top lists. Go for ambiance, service, location, food, activities, rooms, and more. Base your destination on one of those elements, all of them, or something else. Go for ultramodern or classic. Historical luxury has its allure, too.

Try the uncompromising luxury of The Peninsula hotels in Hong Kong or in Beverly Hills, California. Go all out with an experience at what some rank as the top hotel in the world, the all-suite Burj Al Arab, in Dubai, United Arab Emirates. A great hotel exists for every taste and every price range.

UltimateIndulgence:
Forget about the price.

Reality Check:
New high-end hotels often offer low introductory rates to lure travelers from established hotels; hotels may offer discount rates during remodeling. Many of the world's top hotels also may have lower-priced rooms if you just ask.

What It Takes to Get There:

Condé Nast Traveller, www.cntraveller.com; www.concierge.com; www.travelandleisure.com; www.forbes.com/lists; www.tripadvisor.com; www.burj-al-arab.com.

Cost: Acceptable to over the top.

94 Go Down to the Sea
Book a Tall Ship or a Small Ship

Whether you book passage on a tall ship or charter a smaller boat, the exhilaration is the same. With unfurled sails and the rhythm of the wind and sea, sailing lets you kiss stress goodbye.

Turn off the TV and leave the cell phone behind. Bring a book, a hat, and your sunscreen. Join in to hoist the sails or just sit back as the ship heels to the wind and revel in it all.

Try a voyage aboard the *Pride of Baltimore II,* a reproduction of an 1812-era Clipper privateer. Cruise Maine's Penobscot Bay aboard the schooner *Kathryn B* or opt for the ultimate luxury

Above: Relax at the Hotel Hana-Maui and Honua Spa. Right: Sail another ocean on the tall ship *Bluenose II* operated by the Lunenburg Marine Museum Society in Lunenburg, Nova Scotia, Canada.

aboard the *Wind Surf,* complete with computerized sails, pools, spa, and fitness center.

On longer trips, keep a journal, record the sounds, and write a book. Jot down your thoughts on shorter trips, too. They'll conjure great memories years from now.

So hoist the anchor and set sail!

UltimateSail:
Try five-star luxury aboard one of the world's great sailing ships.

Reality Check:
If time or finances limit your opportunities, try finding a shorter trip aboard a tall ship based in a port near you. Even a short trip is an experience.

For example, *Windy I* and *Windy II* sail regularly out of Chicago's Navy Pier.

What It Takes to Get There:
www.smallshipcruises.com;
www.sailingshipadventures.com;
www.windjammer.com;
www.cruiseweb.com.

Cost: Less than $100 for a short local sail; less than $600 for a four-day cruise aboard the *Stad Amsterdam,* and up.

95 The Colossal City
Wander Ancient and Modern Rome

Visitors to this landmark of civilization, the Eternal City of Rome, can almost feel the presence of ancient leaders amid the ancient city's ruins.

Stand among the crumbling pillars of the once-grand Roman Forum; gaze at the great amphitheater, the Colosseum; marvel at the Pantheon; or walk the worn stones of the once-great highway, the Appian Way. And, of course, experience modern Rome, the Vatican, and St. Peter's Square, too.

UltimateRome:
Don't overlook attending Rome's Teatro dell'Opera. The music, the players, the singers, and the setting will awe you. Nonconverts will marvel, too. It's tough not to, especially if you're watching Juliet proclaim her love for Romeo at the sumptuous Teatro dell'Opera or experiencing *Aida* performed in the illuminated ruins of the Baths of Caracalla, the opera's summer home.

Reality Check:
Italy is one of those places you can enjoy whether on a budget or not.

What It Takes to Get There:

www.globusjourneys.com;
www.frommers.com/destinations/rome;
www.transitionsabroad.com;
www.driverinitaly.com;
www.whatsoninrome.com.

Cost: Half-day private tour of Rome, about $250; opera tickets, about $25 to $185 per person depending on season and seats.

96 Nature's Spas
Relax and Enjoy

Soak away your cares in a saltwater thermal pool amid lava fields near the top of the world at Iceland's Blue Lagoon. Or head south and east to slather on the black mud, float in the soothing salt waters, and soak in the sulfur pools of the Dead Sea on the border between Israel and Jordan.

Two very different experiences, yet each represents nature's ultimate health spas.

The Blue Lagoon is a pool of blue-green saltwater near Keflavík. Its geothermal, or naturally heated, water—it's actually cooled before use in the lagoon—has a high concentration of minerals along with silica and blue-green algae that help give it the blue color. With its minerals, salts, and algae, the waters also provide relief for a variety of skin conditions.

The Dead Sea is a world of its own at 1,300 feet below sea level. It even has its own climate as a result of its unique geology. This lowest spot on Earth doesn't teem with fish, either. The water is too salty—so salty that salt deposits cake like mini saline icebergs.

UltimateExperience:
Try both of nature's spas.

Reality Check:
These aren't your average hot tubs in the backyard or at the health spa down the street. Think big as in awesome.

What It Takes to Get There:

Blue Lagoon, www.bluelagoon.is, www.icelandtouristboard.com/bluelagoon, www.exploreiceland.is; Dead Sea, www.inisrael.com, www.deadsea.co.il.

Cost: Blue Lagoon, $21.50 entrance fee for adults or $15 for seniors; Dead Sea resorts, hotel rooms less than $150 a night and up.

Shop without Price Tags
Visit the World's Most Expensive Avenues

Think Rodeo Drive in Beverly Hills; The Magnificent Mile in Chicago; Fifth Avenue in New York; Sloan Street in London; and Rue du Faubourg Saint-Honore and Avenue Montaigne in Paris.

Of course, the task of finding the right shopping area is all the more difficult these days as thousands of small, unique, and expensive boutiques have opened worldwide. Not a bad predicament for the consummate shopper!

These are the days of discounts and outlets, and a sale is always in progress somewhere. As a reward for retirement, instead of the hunting-for-the-bargains routine, why not empower yourself or a loved one to wander along the world's most exclusive shopping streets among glitterati and princesses (princes, too), and actually buy instead of window-shop?

UltimateShopping:
Take in Fashion Week in New York, Milan, or Paris, and order at will.

A Peach of a Beach
Bask in the Sun on the Riviera

The Côte d'Azur is no ordinary vacation spot. Tucked in the south of France, its shores washed by the Mediterranean Sea, the French Riviera regularly plays host to glitterati, bathing beauties, movie stars, high rollers, and kings. Cannes, with its glamorous film festival, and Monte Carlo, with its grand casino, are here. So are magnificent expanses of beach, romantic villas, and gastronomic extravaganzas.

UltimateSightseeing:
Visit during the Cannes Film Festival in mid- to late May and get ready for an eyeful of gawking.

Reality Check:
Crowds are pretty intense during the festival and in the summer months, so make your plans early.

What It Takes to Get There:

www.guideriviera.com; www.rentvillas.com; www.a1vacationproperties.com; www.realadventures.com; www.vacationhomes.com; www.hotels-and-discounts.com, click on Vacation Rentals and follow the links; www.festival-cannes.fr, click on the British flag and then Practical.

Cost: Varies; a villa in the summer on the French Riviera, about $2,700 to $4,500/week; an apartment on the Italian Riviera in summer, about $900/week.

Top left: The Baths of Caracalla is the summer home of the Teatro dell'Opera. Left: Think of the Blue Lagoon as a hot tub on steroids. Top: Umbrellas stack up on the French Riviera at Nice. Above right: Enjoy shopping The Magnificent Mile—North Michigan Avenue in Chicago.

Reality Check:

What's wrong with buying a $2,000 Louis Vuitton bag for half the price?

What It Takes to Get There:

www.discoverfrance.net; www.francetourism.com;
www.themagnificentmile.com;
www.chicagotraveler.com;
www.beverlyhillsbehere.com;
www.fashion-411.com/London, then follow the links;
http://gonyc.about.com/od/shopping.

Cost: Other than travel expenses, it's free except for your purchases.

99 Amore and More
Cruise the Canals of Venice

Share a gondola ride with your true love along the canals of Venice. The moon glistens off the water among the shimmering reflections and lights of the old city.

How much more romantic can it be? Before reclining in the gondola, take a leisurely walk arm-in-arm with your love in Piazza San Marco—famed St. Mark's Square—after a magnificent, sensual meal.

This is Venice, and it's been this way for centuries! Sure, some people complain of overcrowding, tourism, and polluted canal waters, but no other city on Earth is quite like Venice. A visit here can't be duplicated anywhere else.

Marvel at the city's arts and architecture. Tour its churches and squares. Enjoy its cuisine. Watch its artisans blow glass or craft leather, and wander its narrow streets.

UltimateTrip:

Other than just being there, consider taking a gondola home.

Reality Check:

Venice is crowded. Water pollution is an issue, and so is flooding; the city is sinking into the mud. So, you might want to avoid visiting in the summer. Learn about what the city is doing to shore itself up. And the smell? This is Venice.

Italian State Tourist Board, www.enit.it; www.italiantourism.com; www.vacationidea.com and follow the links; www.nationsonline.org and follow the links; more on buying a gondola, www.squero.com, www.tramontingondole.it.

Cost: If you're flexible about where you stay and eat, Italy can be surprisingly inexpensive. If you're not, it's over the top.

00 The Bard's the Thing
Enjoy Shakespeare in London

Relive the world of William Shakespeare, bard of *Romeo and Juliet, The Tempest, The Winter's Tale, Troilus and Cressida,* and so much more, with a trip to Shakespeare's "new" Globe theater, Bankside, Southwark, in London. The re-creation of the 1600s' original open-air Globe is complete with handmade bricks, lime putty, oak laths for the walls, and Norfolk Water Reed on the roof.

The theater is open May through September only. Take in a modern play or one of the classics. Go as a groundling, standing in the yard in front of the stage as was typical in Shakespeare's day, or watch from the gallery for a unique glimpse of past and present as one.

Don't miss the theater's guided tour of Shakespeare's Globe Exhibition.

UltimateStage:
Also catch a performance of the Royal Shakespeare Company in the town of Shakespeare's birth, Stratford-on-Avon, up the road from London.

Reality Check:
Groundlings usually need to bring rain gear in case of foul weather. But it's definitely an experience worth trying. This is theater as it was originally performed.

What It Takes to Get There:
www.goodshow.com; www.shakespeares-globe.org.

Cost: One performance, about $9 to $52.

101 Two (or One) to Tango
Take Lessons in Buenos Aires

Tango has become a dance of the world, from Athens to Boston, Reykjavik to Hollywood, Hamburg to Rio de Janeiro, Warsaw, and beyond. Yet the soul of this sensual dance seems to reverberate with the musical beat of Buenos Aires.

This Argentine coastal city is prime locale for the tango, whether you are participant or spectator. Visit the tango houses, pick up the idea, and then try your hand (and feet) at lessons. The Tourist Information Center in the city or your hotel can

Left: The ambiance of a Venice canal ride is unparalleled. Above: See Shakespearean and modern plays on stage in the new Globe theater modeled after the original open-air Globe of Shakespeare's day.

help you find reputable and reasonable instruction. You may want to take a few lessons from the dance masters—there are many—in the United States before you go.

Think positive, think deliberate, and think passionate about the music and the moves.

UltimateTango:
Keep up your tango through association with any of the many tango clubs and groups across the country.

Reality Check:
As a senior beginner, your moves may not be as extreme as those of young dance stars, but the drama will be equally intense and you'll enjoy the dance just as much.

What It Takes to Get There:
www.planet-tango.com;
http://english.buenosaires.com.

Cost: About $50 for a multilesson package.

102 Drive the Best
Rent a Ferrari

Even ordinary life feels different behind the wheel of a sleek Italian driving machine like a Ferrari.

Choose your color and your model. Hop in and take off. You don't have to be a gearhead (car mechanic or expert) to recognize that this is an incredible experience. The car is hot—0 to 60 mph in 3.95 seconds and with a top speed of 197 mph. Of course, you don't drive at those speeds, but the fact that you can is an amazing feeling.

Unquestionably, this car will get you to your destination quickly and turn plenty of heads along the way. A word of caution: You may want to brush up on your driving skills before getting behind the wheel of this ultramachine.

UltimateToy:
Opt for fire-engine red and then buy it.

Reality Check:
Not to dampen the excitement, but a Ferrari isn't a good choice for off-roading or if you like to maintain a low profile.

What It Takes to Get There:
www.carsfromitaly.com; www.ferrariworld.com;
www.playerscarrental.com;
www.greatexperiencedays.co.uk;
www.ferrariusa.com.

Cost: For purchase, six figures; for rent, about $2,500 a day, but knock off about $1,000 a day if you happen to be in Australia; about $275 an hour in Great Britain.

Top: Tango your time away in Brazil. Above: A Ferrari circa any year is an experience to drive. Right: Nix those hotel reservation headaches on your cross-country trip with an RV.

Sightseeing

Your Home Away from Home
See the USA in an RV

Even if the idea of driving around the country doesn't have instant appeal, you may want to rethink the advantages of RV life. Hotel over-bookings and checkouts, long airport check-in and security lines, and lost luggage are no longer your hassles. When you take to the road in your personal travel craft, pack your things and forget your troubles; stop and go when the spirit moves you; and make friends with great people from everywhere.

Head south for spring training, then north to your favorite lake in the summer, or cruise leisurely to the nation's capital for cherry blossom time, and then west to see the colors of the high-mountain fall foliage. Just pack up the RV, pick up the keys, and drive. Alternatively, leave the RV packed and take off on a whim.

RV options are endless, from small, towable pop-up and truck campers to luxurious motor homes that sleep eight easily. Rent or buy, new or used, the choices are yours.

UltimateRVing:
Travel with your Airstream trailer. Their smaller size lets you go almost anywhere.

Reality Check:
RV life isn't for everyone. Quarters are compact, especially if you're traveling with company. A strategy to circumvent the too-close-for-comfort complaint is to plan short trips and occasionally opt for a hotel room.

What It Takes to Get There:

Recreation Vehicle Industry Association, www.rvia.org; Recreation Vehicle Rental Association, www.rvra.org; Kampgrounds of America, www.koa.com, and www.koakampgrounds.com/rvfinder; www.cruiseamerica.com; www.adventuretouring.com.

Cost: New and used models are available to fit any budget; new small pop-ups, about $4,000 to $13,000, bigger models more than $140,000; rentals from less than $100 a night; equipment, mileage, and insurance charges may be extra; often multiple-night rental discounts available.

104 Branching Out
Stay in a Tree House

Literally. These homes among the branches are hardly the ramshackle tree houses of your childhood fun and games in the backyard.

Today's versions generally are state-of-the-art platform homes in exotic or unusual locales such as the cliffs of California's Big Sur, remote Africa,

along the coastline of the South China Sea, or in the dense forests surrounding Washington's Mount Rainer. A sojourn to the latter gives new meaning to "head in the clouds."

They can get a bit rustic, however, depending on the locale and the level of accommodations. They also can enfold you in over-the-top luxury, so research your trip or sojourn thoroughly.

UltimatePerch:
Stay in tree houses around the world.

Reality Check:
This is not a good vacation idea for people who sleepwalk.

What It Takes to Get There:

www.postranchinn.com;
www.adventurelandtravel.com and look for unusual lodging; www.treehousesofhawaii.com;
http://cedarcreektreehouse.com;
www.places.co.za, then type in Zululand Tree Lodge.

Cost: $250/night, home in the cedars overlooking Mount Rainer; 5-star hotel version of a tree house at Post Ranch Inn in Big Sur, $795/night.

105 Heavenly Fireworks
See the Northern Lights

Nature creates few heavenly canvases that match the aura of the northern lights. Imagine giant air-brushed spirals and rivers of white swirled across the dark night sky.

Also known as the aurora borealis, this highly charged molecular event is unparalleled. The northern lights sometimes are visible from the northern United States in summer, although the best view is from north of the Arctic Circle in

winter, around midnight, and at the new moon when the sky is darkest.

Predicting when the northern lights will be the most dramatic is high science that involves the National Weather Service's Space Environment Center, geomagnetic activity on Earth, the "weather" in space, solar activity, and more.

UltimateFireworks:
Check out what the experts say about when and where the viewing is best. Those experts include the Geophysical Institute, University of Alaska—you can sign up for its Aurora Alert—and the Space Environment Center.

Reality Check:
This can be cold-weather entertainment if you opt for a winter trip. Be sure to spend the extra money for proper clothing. Rentals usually are available.

What It Takes to Get There:
Geophysical Institute, University of Alaska–Fairbanks, www.gi.alaska.edu/ then click on Aurora Forecast; Space Environment Center, http://sec.noaa.gov/; www.auroraborealisyukon.com; www.alaskatours.com, click on Winter Tours.

Cost: About $500 for a two-day, two-night tour; winter clothing rental, add about $90.

The Crown Jewels of Parks
Visit Yellowstone and Glacier National Parks

The debate rages. Some say Yellowstone, the expansive 2.2-million-acre granddaddy of national parks, is the best. Other visitors insist that

---

Left: Post Ranch Inn at Big Sur offers high-end tree-house luxury. Top: The aurora borealis lights the Northern sky. Above: A plume signals Old Faithful's display at Yellowstone.

Montana's dramatic Glacier National Park is the most magnificent.

We've all grown up with images of Yellowstone—the geyser, Old Faithful (one of 250 in the park) letting off steam regularly, Mammoth Hot Springs looking like a scene from a sci-fi thriller, and, of course, the Lower Falls of the Grand Canyon of Yellowstone.

Glacier, on Montana's border with Canada, was a well-kept secret, although today it's almost as popular as Yellowstone. Across the border is Waterton Lakes National Park, and together they make up Waterton-Glacier International Peace Park.

Both Glacier and Yellowstone are natural jewels that offer nature at its best whether you prefer mountains, water, flora, or fauna.

UltimatePark:

Try visiting both of these magnificent parks.

Reality Check:

Parts of these parks can get pretty crowded during the summer. About 4,400 people work in Yellowstone! Consider going off-season or see the less-traveled areas.

What It Takes to Get There:

www.yellowstone.net; www.nps.gov/glac; www.gutsytraveler.com; www.canyoncalling.com.

Cost: Six days in Yellowstone and Tetons, about $1,850, Canyon Calling Adventures for Women; park admission, Golden Age Passport, lifetime pass to national parks for ages 62 and older, $10.

107 The Old and the Mighty
Walk among California's Giant Sequoias

These largest trees on Earth dwarf man and his machines. Standing next to General Sherman—the most massive of the trees—a man looks like a beetle, his SUV a small toy. The tree weighs more than 2,000 tons, and its bark is up to three feet thick!

Giant Sequoia National Park in Northern California's Sierra Nevada mountain range is home to these massive and magnificent elder statesmen of life. Some are more than 3,000 years old, wider than a city street and more than 270 feet tall, higher than many office buildings.

UltimateTree:

Stay in the park for its full effect.

Reality Check:

The giant sequoias are impressive but are located in only a small portion of Sequoia National Park and neighboring Kings Canyon National Park. Go for much more than simply to see the trees.

What It Takes to Get There:

www.americansouthwest.net, follow the links; http://nationalparkreservations.com; www.nps.gov/seki/index.htm; www.fs.fed.us/r5/sequoia; www.riverdeep.net, type "sequoia" into search engine.

Cost: Wuksachi Lodge in Sequoia National Park, $80 to $185/night.

108 House of the Rising Sun
Watch from Maui's Mount Haleakala

The sun's light explodes above the dark crater rim illuminating what looks like the surface of the moon. It's almost as if you were standing on the moon—dark, barren lava rocks jutting toward a sky flaming with brilliant colors as the new day dawns. It's a sharp contrast to the brilliant blue waters, lush green tropical landscape, and jagged black lava cliffs 10,023 feet below. It's the top of the world, or so it seems.

Standing atop Maui's Mount Haleakala at sunrise is breathtaking. This is the not-so-familiar yet incredible picture postcard of this island's tropical paradise.

Haleakala means "house of the sun." It's not really a crater, though it looks like one and definitely feels like it, too.

UltimateSunrise:

Hitch a ride up, watch the sunrise, hike or bike for hours, then return to the beach to relax your weary bones. This is living.

Reality Check:

To be there for sunrise requires getting up long before the sun rises, so be prepared.

What It Takes to Get There:

Friends of Haleakala National Park, www.fhnp.org; www.tripadvisor.com; www.greathawaiivacations.com.

Cost: The view is free.

109 Lazy River Days
Take a Paddle Wheeler

Mud-clouded waters lap the passing shore. The methodical drone of generators mixes with the sound of churning water from the giant paddle wheel as the steamer makes its way down the mighty Mississippi River. It's a scene right out of Mark Twain's novel *Huckleberry Finn.*

Left: A giant sequoia heads skyward in Northern California. Above: The sunrise is nothing short of magnificent from Maui's Mount Haleakala.

Welcome to your modern-day passage aboard a paddle wheeler bound for wherever on whatever river. In this case, it's the *Delta Queen* embarked from St. Paul, Minnesota, and bound for St. Louis, Missouri, and stops in between. This is a page from your memory book, not Huck Finn's.

Enjoy calliope music, sumptuous food, and first-class service on your slow meander. The trip includes stops along the way at what today may be out-of-the-way towns, although in Huck's day they were bustling river centers.

The lifestyle is contagious. Once you try it, look for adventure on other North American rivers as well as elsewhere in the world. Make it a short jaunt or a long journey. The choice is yours.

UltimatePassage:
Try fall foliage along the Missouri or the route of Lewis and Clark along the Columbia.

Reality Check:
This is about lifestyle, not speed.

What It Takes to Get There:

www.uncommonjourneys.com;
www.empressofthenorth.com;
www.americanweststeamboat.com;
www.steamboats.org; www.deltaqueen.com.

Cost: $795 and up for the *Delta Queen;* about $3,840 for seven-night Lewis-and-Clark cruise.

110 American Heritage
Attend a Native American Powwow

This modern link to the ancient culture and spirit of Native Americans provides a powerful connection to the past for those who participate and those who view it.

Powwows draw tribes from across North America and guests from around the world to share dances, singing, culture, and the traditions and

Above: Head back to the river days of Huck Finn aboard a paddle wheeler. Top right: Native Americans have a unique heritage to share. Right: Waikiki Beach is the spot to soak in sun, sand, sea, and sunsets.

spirit of Native American peoples. It's a social gathering, too, often with competitions and marketplaces.

The annual Gathering of Nations, for example, can draw representatives from 500 tribes and even holds a Miss Indian World competition.

UltimateHeritage:
Take the time and make the effort to understand the traditions of the indigenous peoples of North America.

Reality Check:
You are a guest in another culture. Pay attention to its customs and protocols.

What It Takes to Get There:
www.shadowwolf.org;
www.snowwowl.com;
www.gatheringofnations.com;
www.drumbeatindianarts.com;
www.travelnow.com.

Cost: Admission cost varies, free and up.

Sunset Sensation
Watch It from Waikiki

The fiery orange and pink tropical sky above the shimmering cool blue Pacific Ocean may be one of the most beautiful sunsets on Earth.

Waikiki Beach generally conjures up images of tanned surfers, crowded beaches, and bathing beauties, but that all pales in comparison to this magnificent canvas from nature.

See it from the private lanai of your condo, the veranda of a hotel, or from the beachside dining room of the venerable pink Royal Hawaiian Hotel. Built in the early 1900s on the site that once was the playground of Hawaiian royalty, this historic hotel remains a unique and special place to visit, stay, or simply enjoy. Try an outdoor dinner with sunset as your appetizer.

UltimateSunset:
That's your call. But worth mentioning, watch it from the jetty off Fort DeRussy. The last bits of the sun slip off the horizon to the haunting sounds of taps.

Reality Check:
This is paradise.

What It Takes to Get There:
www.fodors.com; www.planet-hawaii.com;
www.greathawaiivacations.com.

Cost: The sunset is free.

112 America's Ultimate Majesty
Visit the Grand Canyon

One of the Seven Natural Wonders of the World, the Grand Canyon is nature at its most magnificent and surreal. This is the place of dreams. Jagged chasms ten miles wide cut through towering red mesas. A mile below, the massive Colorado River snakes across the sunken desert.

Live the picture postcard. Stay at a lodge on the canyon's rim, hike the trails that cling to tiered cliffs (or ride them via burro), camp beside the river, run the rapids, and explore eons of history etched into the canyon.

UltimateCanyon:

Experienced hikers can try a rim-to-river-to-rim five-day trek. That's 10,000 feet of altitude change.

Reality Check:

Seeing the deepest canyon on Earth is a take-your-breath-away experience—and the world knows it. Crowds can be intense, so book early and consider going off-season. Also, be prepared for the weather and the altitude. Temperatures on the canyon floor can reach 120 degrees.

What It Takes to Get There:

www.nps.gov/grca or www.grandcanyonchamber.org; Grand Canyon Railway from Williams, Arizona, www.thetrain.com.

Costs: All types of lodging, transportation, and trips available; rates vary vastly.

113 From Sea to Shining Sea
Visit America

From the mountains to the prairies, deserts, forests, and from sea to shining sea, the United States has it all. This is a country of cultural and ethnic differences, too.

Use your retirement to discover as many aspects of America as possible by visiting all 50 states or a select few. Travel by car, bus, train, or plane—even bicycle or motorcycle.

The experiences, lessons in history, and interactions with people will be well worth the effort.

UltimateTour:
Visit all 50 states.

Reality Check:
Go beyond the big cities and be sure to take the time to see many of the unusual and sometimes extraordinary memorials to life and history. Try an Amtrak rail pass.

What It Takes to Get There:
From the Travel Industry Association of America, www.seeamerica.org; www.travelnotes.org, click on North America; www.exchangehomesoia.com; www.bootsnall.com, click on North America; www.americanorientexpress.com.

Cost: Amtrak rail pass, about $185 to $550.

Veterans may reconnect with their unit's association and travel to past battlegrounds, or travel individually or with loved ones to share those places and memories—sometimes to make peace with the past.

Times have changed, and travel to distant lands reflects that. Take a motorcycle up the Ho Chi Minh Trail in Vietnam. Stay at the Sheraton Hotel in Saigon. Visit a bustling and modern Seoul, South Korea, or stand on the beaches of Normandy in France.

UltimateMemory:
Leave a new legacy—work with orphans and children or donate to the community.

Reality Check:
Remember the past but embrace the future.

What It Takes to Get There:
www.discovermekong.com; www.military.com; www.ussearch.com; www.militarylocator.com; www.vetfriends.com; www.vets.org; California Pacific Tours, www.cptours.com; www.valortours.com; www.abc.net/directory/Society/Military/Veterans; www.go4travel.com.

Cost: Varies, a ten-day tour to Korea, about $2,350; about $600 for a nine-day Vietnam tour; Sheraton Saigon, $140 to $350 a night.

War Memories and Memorials
Return to Where You Served

Veterans frequently lose contact with the people and places from their years in the service. The chasms of time and space are just too broad. But as we age, the curiosity to find lost friends and see lost places often returns.

Left: Thrill to the vistas of the Grand Canyon. Top: Point your compass and venture across America.
Above: Pause to remember those who sacrificed their lives.

What It Takes to Get There:

Search "Google" with keywords Travel and Battlefields, then click on Google Directory; www.battlefieldtours.co.uk; www.valortours.com; www.kingsheadadventures.com; www.gettysburg.com; www.globusjourneys.com.

Cost: Varies, depending on location; about $1,000 to $2,900 for Normandy tour; $800 to $1,300 for World War I battlefield tour in a 4x4.

115 Heroics of the Past
Visit History's Great Battlefields

The great battlefields of the world chronicle historical change throughout the millennia.

Stand at the sites of hard-fought battles and great bravery—the Waterloo of Napoleon's demise; Verdun from World War I; Gettysburg of the Civil War; Iwo Jima and Midway, decisive Pacific island battles of World War II, and, of course, Normandy, site of D-day, 1944.

Opt for older battlefields or newer ones. Take these opportunities to brush up on the history and literature of the battles, the wars, and the people of times past.

UltimateBattle:
Visit the sites of some of the bloodiest battles that today are serenely beautiful.

Reality Check:
Urbanization has encroached on many older battlefields that no longer exist. But to stand at or near the site of a historic battle can carry electricity that's worth the trip.

116 Eiffel Tower Power
Explore the City of Lights

Perhaps one of the world's most famous images is the Eiffel Tower. Built as a revolutionary example of engineering prowess for the 1889 World's Fair, it climbs 984 feet into the Parisian sky.

That's not high by skyscraper standards, but who goes to the Eiffel Tower strictly for the view? Paris, after all, is the city of romance, art, and beauty, and this is its pinnacle. See it by day or lit by night. Take your spouse to the top and propose all over again, or pledge your love to a significant other.

Of course, while you're there, don't miss Paris's other attractions, from the Bastille to Montmartre, Saint Germain des Pres, Place de La Concorde, Champs-Elysées, Arc de Triomphe, and Notre Dame. The list continues. A walk along the River Seine is a must, too.

UltimateParis:
Visit Paris again and again. You'll see something new every time.

Reality Check:
Don't miss the Paris Flea Market.

What It Takes to Get There:

www.aboutparisvacations.com;
www.ecityrama.com;
www.frenchexperience.com;
www.discoverfrance.net;
www.paris-eiffel-tower-news.com.

Cost: Eiffel Tower, from about $12; one-day Paris museum pass, about $23.

All Aboard
Ride the Train across Europe

Rail travel in Europe is the equivalent of car or airline travel in the United States. It's the easiest way to get from point A to point B. The rail system is fast, efficient, and dependable—and a bargain to boot. It's also easy to navigate.

Top left: Colonel Sandy Colburn, a Civil War aide to General G. B. McClellan of Virginia, strikes a pose circa 1862.
Above: The Eiffel Tower towers above the Seine River in Paris.

Remember the Eurail pass you may have used as a youth to travel from London to Ostend, Brussels, Paris, Rome, Vienna, and beyond? Variations of it still are available today. If you've never had the pleasure of experiencing the sights, sounds, tastes, and feel of Europe, this is your chance to tour via a fabulous system of trains. They literally will take you anywhere.

UltimateTrack:

A ride aboard the legendary Venice-Simplon Orient Express. This is no ordinary train. No take-out dining on paper and Styrofoam or riding in uncomfortable rows. Travelers on this train experience fine wines and haute cuisine, fine linens, china, crystal, and more.

Reality Check:

Europe's trains run on time.

What It Takes to Get There:

Senior discounts, www.bootsnall.com; www.raileurope.com.

Cost: Eurail passes, under $100 and up, depending on travel class, countries visited, and travel frequency; Orient Express, Venice-Prague-Paris-London, about $3,000, Paris-Vienna-Budapest, about $1,900.

118 The Wall of Walls
Walk the Great Wall of China

Massive, seemingly endless, this is not an ordinary stone wall. It's broad—you can hike or bike atop it, and it seems to stretch forever. The Great Wall is not one wall but several, and all were built at different times by various emperors as fortifications against warring tribes and enemies.

The exact date construction began is tough to pinpoint, but it was believed to be at least several centuries BC. The wall that you see today comes primarily from the Ming dynasty (around 1368–1644).

A day tour is an easy jaunt from Beijing.

UltimateOrientation:

Make the Great Wall part of a longer journey to learn about Chinese culture and history.

Reality Check:

Study Chinese history first to maximize your visit and better understand the truly unique characteristics of the Chinese people and culture.

What It Takes to Get There:

www.explorient.com;
www.china-hiking.com;
www.chinadiscoveries.com;
www.chinahighlights.com;
www.travelchina.com.

Above: Try train travel with all its comforts and glory. Top right: China's Great Wall seems to stretch on forever. Right: Kilauea's lava flows on the island of Hawaii.

Cost: 14 to 17 days, including the Great Wall, about $2,600 to $3,300; seniors tour, about $1,200, excluding airfare.

Go with the Lava Flow
Visit an Active Volcano

Watch firsthand a tiny sample of the violence and fury that rips the Earth and builds and destroys continents.

See Java's Semeru, Italy's Etna and Stromboli, Hawaii's Kilauea, Washington's St. Helens, or Mexico's Colima. The list goes on. If there's a spot on the globe you're thinking of visiting, a volcano may not be too far away.

Tour groups not only will take you to see these volcanoes but often feature study tours as well. Tours in Italy, for example, offer a perfect opportunity to see active volcanoes like Etna and Stromboli, as well as the destruction and rebirth caused by past volcanoes like Vesuvius, which erupted in 79 AD and destroyed the Roman city of Pompeii.

For volcano-philes, the Weekly Volcanic Activity Report from the Smithsonian and U.S. Geological Survey will keep you abreast of what's up in the world of volcanoes.

UltimateEruption:
Be there when it happens.

Reality Check:
If you opt to trek an active volcano on your own, check with local authorities first about current activity and pay attention to warnings. It could save your life.

What It Takes to Get There:

http://volcano.und.edu; Weekly Volcanic Activity Report, www.volcano.si.edu/reports/usgs; www.volcanodiscovery.com.

Cost: Varies, a two-week tour of Italy's volcanoes, about $3,100 to $3,350; from Krakatoa to Bali in Indonesia, about $2,800.

120 ## Will Wonders Never Cease
See the Wonders of the World

Setting a retirement goal of visiting the Seven Wonders of the World builds great latitude into your travel plans. The reason: Several wonders lists exist, and not all of the wonders themselves still exist.

Do you favor the Seven Wonders of the Ancient World? The Great Pyramid of Giza in Egypt is one of those stops. But such wonders as the Hanging Gardens of Babylon, the Temple of Artemis at Ephesus, the Statue of Zeus at Olympia, and the Colossus of Rhodes unfortunately no longer exist.

Outdoor types may prefer the Seven Natural Wonders that include Mount Everest, the Great Barrier Reef, Victoria Falls, and, closer to home, the northern lights and the Grand Canyon. An alternative to consider are the Seven Underwater Wonders, including the Galapagos Islands, the Great Barrier Reef, Lake Baikal, the Deep-Sea Vents, and Palau.

The Seven Wonders of the Modern World, which also are worthy destinations, include the Empire State Building, Itaipu Dam, CN Tower, Panama Canal, Channel Tunnel, North Sea Protection Works, and the Golden Gate Bridge.

Pick one list or something from each one. To start planning your itinerary, see a version of a complete list online at the Wonderclub.

For an unreal peek at some of the wonders, virtually visit the Unmuseum.

UltimateWonder:
See every single one, of course.

Reality Check:
Don't be surprised if not everyone agrees with your Wonders of the World list.

What It Takes to Get There:

www.sevenwondersworld.com;
www.wonderclub.com, then click on World Wonders;
the Unmuseum, www.unmuseum.org/wonders.htm.

Cost: Varies, depending on the wonder.

Don't miss the Hermitage, home to an incredibly massive art collection, in St. Petersburg, Russia.

Prague, with its abundant spires, is a vibrant Westernized city and popular tourist destination. Cruise the Vltava River. See the Old Jewish Quarter, St. Vitus Cathedral, and Wenceslas Square.

Consider visiting some of the literally hundreds of historic castles in Hungary.

UltimateVisit:
Take an extended river cruise from point to point.

Reality Check:
In some regions, the big cities may be highly Westernized and thriving, yet some places outside the metropolitan areas are truly like Third World countries.

What It Takes to Get There:
www.travelciti.com, www.vacationrentals.com, then follow the links to the city of your choice; www.petersburg-russia.com; www.cityrealtyrussia.com, follow the links; www.steinbecktravel.com; www.budapesthotels.com.

Cost: About $1,200 for airfare and three nights' hotel, Prague; $60 and up, St. Petersburg apartment, hotels, about $75 a night and up; Budapest four-star hotel, about $76 to $320 a night.

21 Behind the Iron Curtain
Tour Eastern Europe and Beyond

For a truly memorable and impressionable experience, see Eastern Europe and states of the former Soviet Union. The history, the culture, and the people will amaze almost anyone who grew up during the Cold War. See Moscow, St. Petersburg, Prague, Budapest, Nuremburg, Krakow, and other fabled cities.

Moscow, rather than the mysterious city of James Bond intrigue, is a fabulous combination of Vienna and Paris mixed with Russian culture. Trench coats are conspicuously absent. The Kremlin isn't a building but a walled city. Red Square, except for its massive nature and the conspicuous, onion-domed St. Basil's Cathedral, could be anywhere.

122 Priceless
Visit the World's Great Art Museums

What are the world's finest art museums? Although art experts' opinions may vary, the real answer depends on your tastes and travels. Art truly does reside in the eyes of the beholder. Why not indulge your art appreciation by visiting some great repositories of the great masters?

Left: Victoria Falls on Zimbabwe's Zambezi River is a Natural Wonder of the World. Above: The distinct domes of St. Basil's Cathedral rise from one end of Red Square in Moscow.

No matter the genre or artists you prefer, the Louvre in Paris tops most lists. Go beyond the *Mona Lisa,* though; her enigmatic smile is only a tiny part of a collection of fabulous art.

Other possibilities on your list may include the Musée d'Orsay in Paris; Tate Gallery in England; Metropolitan Museum of Art and Museum of Modern Art in New York City; the State Hermitage Museum in St. Petersburg, Russia; the Ufizzi in Florence, Italy; Chicago Art Institute; Tokyo National Museum; Taipei Fine Arts Museum; and the National Gallery of Art in Washington, D.C.

UltimateAppreciation:

Plan your visits to one museum at a time and turn these trips into art-appreciation getaways.

Reality Check:

It would take a lifetime and then some to really see all there is.

What It Takes to Get There:

Art Museum Network, www.amn.org;
www.artcyclopedia.com,
click on Art Museums Worldwide;
www.netpopular.com, then check art for listing
of many of the top museums.

Cost: Varies. Special exhibits sometimes cost extra.

Above: Enjoy the Art Institute of Chicago. Top right: The Antoni Gaudí–designed Sagrada Familia dominates the Barcelona, Spain, skyline. Right: A carriage driver and his horse share a moment in Vienna, Austria.

Spread out your visits to these architectural tributes to religion. Seeing too many at once can be overwhelming and often dims the true magnificence of each marvel.

What It Takes to Get There:

www.gate1travel.com; www.tripadvisor.com; www.sacredplaces.org; www.vacationstoindia.com; UNESCO World Heritage Centre, http://whc.unesco.org.

Cost: Varies depending on where you go.

23 Built for Glory
Be Awed by Religious Architecture

Visit the world's greatest cathedrals, temples, synagogues, and mosques. Many, especially outside the United States, are true architectural marvels—at the time of their construction as well as today—and great tributes to their respective religions.

Gaze at one of the most famous stained-glass windows in the world at Notre Dame in Paris. See the famous onion domes of St. Basil's in Moscow's Red Square. Take in the sumptuousness of St. Peter's Basilica at the Vatican in Rome. Marvel at Istanbul's Blue Mosque with its six minarets and blue tiles. Enjoy the history of St. Vitus Cathedral in Prague. Visit the huge cathedral in Seville, Spain, the monuments of Nara in Japan, the Dome of the Rock in Jerusalem, and other religious edifices.

UltimateEclecticism:
Visit the monuments of several religions.

124 Vienna Rhapsody
Waltz through the City of Culture

Think of Vienna as a city possessed by music, arts, architecture, and excitement.

See the treasures of its palaces, inside and out. The architecture throughout the city is unforgettable. Don't miss the magnificence of the Wiener Staatsoper, or State Opera House. Built in 1869, it's still home to performances and the Vienna Opera Ball.

While you're at it, enjoy Vienna's great amusement park, the Prater. Its giant Ferris wheel was built in 1897. Take in the Schönbrunn Palace, the Spanish Riding School (home of the Lippizan horses), and, of course, a performance of the Vienna Boys Choir, which traces its origins back more than 500 years.

Get a taste of Vienna and Austrian culture in the United States by attending the Viennese Opera Ball in New York, presented under the auspices of the U.S.–Austrian Chamber of Commerce.

UltimateVienna:

Visit in December and enjoy the Christmas markets as well as the balls.

Reality Check:

Plan to spend plenty of time in Vienna because there's plenty to do.

What It Takes to Get There:

www.viennaticket.com; www.viennaticketoffice.com; http://vienneseoperaball.com; www.venere.com; www.viennacitytourist.com.

Cost: Varies, a three-star hotel, about $70 and up/night; Vienna Opera Ball, admission about $265, with seating additional, tickets as low as $15 to dress rehearsal, standing room only; Vienna Boys Choir performance, about $44 and up.

125 Sealed in Time
See the Ruins of Pompeii

The Roman city of Pompeii, a short distance southeast of Naples, Italy, is an eerie canvas of life sealed in time against a backdrop of its destroyer, the volcano Mount Vesuvius. When the mountain

erupted in 79 AD, its ash and lava trapped many of the city's 20,000 people in their tracks, burying them along with their entire city.

Life stopped. Artwork, lifestyles, homes, the public forum, and more were preserved so that today visitors get an insider portrait of Roman life in the first century AD. The realism of it all hits home, too, in the terror on the faces of the victims, preserved in plaster casts. A cast of a dog's last struggles is perhaps one of the most well-known.

Be sure to see the ruins of Herculaneum, a smaller seaside city also buried under yards and yards of ash by Vesuvius's eruption.

UltimateItaly:

Wander Pompeii for several days and then enjoy much more of Italy. Try a taste of Italy on the cheap and then upscale, too. Both sides are uniquely fun.

Reality Check:

If the ruins of Pompeii interest you, try a visit to ruins in Turkey, such as those at Ephesus.

www.touritaly.org;
www.globusjourneys.com;
http://goitaly.about.com.

Cost: About $6 to visit Pompeii; combined with an 11-day trip that includes Rome, Venice, and Florence, about $1,900.

26 A Taste of Antiquity
Visit the Acropolis in Athens

It's easy to see why the ancient gods chose Greece as their home. The hills dotted with white-washed buildings set against azure blue waters of the Ionian Sea and jagged lush cliffs draw modern-day visitors, too. The fun-loving, friendly people, sensational food, and delightful music and dance crown the experience.

Cruise, drive, or do both to the fabulous Greek Isles. Visit Athens old and new. Wander the old streets of the Plaka and gaze at *the* image from ancient history, the ruins of the Parthenon atop the Acropolis. Better still, get up close to this image of antiquity. Or visit the ultramodern Olympic Stadium in Athens, built for the 2004 Games. Take a side trip to Mount Olympus, home of the ancient gods, or visit Olympia, the birthplace of the Olympic Games, and stand where the first Olympians stood. Wherever you travel in Greece, you'll see ruins of its extraordinary civilization.

UltimateGreece:
Cruise the Greek Isles; don't miss an always memorable donkey ride up the hillside on Patmos or Rhodes. It's touristy, but it's a great tale to recount.

Reality Check:
A 2-day stop on a 14-day world trip doesn't do Greece justice. This place is meant to be a destination trip.

What It Takes to Get There:

www.athens2004.com; www.gogreece.com; Hellenic Ministry of Culture, www.culture.gr; http://www.travelling.gr/cruises; www.adventurewomen.com.

Cost: Less than $50 for a day cruise and up; five days cruising and sightseeing, about $5,700 (Adventure Women).

Top left: Plaster casts on display in Pompeii reveal some of the horror of victims when Mount Vesuvius erupted in 79 AD.
Above: The ruins of the Erechtheion are among the buildings that grace the Acropolis in Athens.

127 The Irish Gift of Gab
Kiss the Blarney Stone

According to tradition, those who kiss the Blarney Stone receive the gift of eloquence. Those who seek eloquence may have to settle for gazing at the stone, instead.

The fabled stone is high on a parapet of the 15th century Blarney Castle, and to actually kiss it requires some physical maneuvering that may be a bit much for most. Some people opt to hang upside down or dangle over an abyss. Another option: Kiss the virtual Blarney Stone at www.irelandseye.com/blarney.

Beyond Blarney Castle, which tops a cliff in southwestern Ireland, lies the popular village of Blarney, beautiful countryside, and the larger city of Cork, which is nearby.

UltimateIrish:

If your heritage is Irish, visit the village of your ancestors.

Reality Check:

Cork can be an expensive city. It's also crowded in the summer, so consider a visit off-season.

What It Takes to Get There:

www.blarneycastle.ie; www.eurovacations.com, click on Cork, Ireland; www.go-today.com, then follow the links to Cork, Ireland.

Cost: Two nights, about $150, excluding airfare.

128 Island Hopping
Journey the Seven Seas

Think islands as a retirement goal. Then get ready to sample a world of diverse cultures and geography.

Experience the mysteries of Easter Island. Cruise the Galapagos, a natural phenomenon of isolation in today's highly developed world. Sail among the Northern Mariana Islands, a commonwealth of the United States in the Pacific, and include a climb atop Suicide Hill on the lush island of Saipan, site of a bloody World War II battle. Stop on Guam, a U.S. territory that's a gateway to the Far East and home to several big military bases.

Opt for the Canary Islands, Spanish islands off the coast of Morocco. Taipei is another don't miss. Don't stop there, either. Try Tonga, Aruba, Nauru,

Above: Blarney Castle is north of Cork in southern Ireland. Top right: A moai stands silently at Rano Raraku quarry on Easter Island. Right: Picture the idyllic life aboard a barge in Holland.

Turks and Caicos, Falkland Islands, Prince Edward Island, Zanzibar, and Bonaire, to name just a few of the world's communities and countries surrounded by water.

UltimateHop:

Don't be afraid to go out of the way. If you're looking for more travel ideas, check out the islands directory, www.island-search.com.

Reality Check:

Be sure to pack your bug spray and sunscreen. It may sound exotic to camp on a distant beach or hike the jungles and rain forests, but mosquitoes often abound.

What It Takes to Get There:

50plus Expeditions, www.50plusexpeditions.com; www.hillmanwonders.com; www.tripadvisor.com; http://homeamericanexpress.com; www.island-search.com; www.kontiki.org.

Cost: Eight-day Galapagos cruise, about $900 land only. Adding the transportation to get there skyrockets the cost; Canary Islands, three-star hotel, from about $128/night; Taipei, about $1,990 and up.

Take a River Cruise
Enjoy the Waters of Europe and Beyond

From the Danube to the Elbe, the Rhine, Seine, Yangtze, and beyond, journey across Europe and its neighbors via its waterways. The cruising expe-

rience provides a unique way to take in the history, ambiance, culture, and cuisine of many different worlds.

Take local ferries, boats, and barges, or try upscale cruise lines.

Try the Volga, Moscow to St. Petersburg, past medieval cities. Take a day cruise along the Seine to experience a new view of Paris. Try a cruise in Western luxury on the Yangtze, complete with English-speaking guides and haute cuisine. Experience the legendary Danube.

UltimateRivers:

Take several different cruises to appreciate each river's uniqueness.

Reality Check:

Some cruise lines offer discounted airfare packages for those booking their cruises.

What It Takes to Get There:

www.vikingrivercruises.com; www.friendlyplanet.com; www.globusjourneys.com; www.trip-quest.com, and choose cruise specials; www.iexplore.com.

Cost: 9-night all-inclusive China cruise tour, under $2,000 and up; 7-night cruise, Holland and Belgium, under $1,000; 12 days Nuremburg to Budapest, about $1,875.

130 Gateway to Asia
Visit Hong Kong

East truly meets West in this international city of the Far East. Taste colonial Great Britain as you sip tea at the Peninsula Hotel. Experience modern-day China in Hong Kong's marketplaces. Take the *Star Ferry* across the harbor. See the New Territories and Kowloon. Beijing is a mere 30-hour express train ride west.

And, in case you think Hong Kong is too Far East for your taste, Walt Disney just opened Hong Kong Disneyland! There's something for everyone here.

Don't miss the Hong Kong shopping experience, either. You'll find everything from hand-tailored suits and shirts to wonderful artwork.

Great Britain returned Hong Kong and the New Territories to the Chinese in 1997, yet Hong Kong remains a capitalistic connection to the West.

UltimateHongKong:
See the harbor at night.

Reality Check:
The city is thriving and international, but it's still part of China.

What It Takes to Get There:
www.hongkongdisneyland.com;
http://homeamericanexpress.com;
www.travelciti.com, and click on Vacation Deals.

Cost: As inexpensive or as high-end as you choose; five-star hotel, three nights including air-fare, from $1,470.

131 Land of the Pharaohs
Gaze at Giza and Other Pyramids

For eons, monuments to ancient leaders and civilizations have stood guard among the shifting sands of Egypt. Some of those monuments have given up secrets to the past. Others, long-since victims of tomb raiders, weather, and more, have kept some of their secrets hidden for millennia.

Experience Ancient Egypt by seeing its remnants. But don't expect Indiana Jones or Lara Croft to emerge. This isn't Hollywood; it's the real thing.

See the Temple of Ramses at Abu Simbal; the Valley of the Kings at Luxor, where more than 60 pharaohs have their tombs; the Pyramids of Giza and the mysterious Sphinx.

UltimateEgypt:
Combine an extended Nile River luxury cruise with a land package to allow plenty of time to see the pyramids, Sphinx, temples, museums, and more.

Reality Check:
Don't miss the Aswan Dam.

What It Takes to Get There:
www.friendlyplanet.com;
www.worldhoteltravel.com/destinations/Egypt;
www.touregypt.net.

Cost: Ten-day land/river package, about $2,000 and up.

standing at the gates of Buckingham Palace? They march whenever the guard is changed— either once a day or every other day, depending on the season—and always to a band. It's like a mini-Macy's parade. Come early to get a good spot along the railing and enjoy.

UltimateGuard:

Be there for the Trooping of the Color, the celebration of the queen's official birthday in June.

Reality Check:

Admittedly, it's a tourist attraction, but what's a trip to London without seeing Big Ben and the changing of the guard at Buckingham Palace!

What It Takes to Get There:

www.londontown.com;
http://away.com, then follow the links to United Kingdom; www.123London.com;
www.pilotguides.com.

Cost: Free.

London Landmarks
Changing of the Guard

Experience the pomp and pageantry of castles and kings. See the changing of the Queen's Guard at Buckingham Palace in London. It's only a ceremony, but it's recognizable living history.

Do you have childhood memories of the pictures of these stern, never-smiling soldiers in their flaming red tunics and tall, black bearskin caps

Top left: Hong Kong mixes ancient and modern cultures. Top: For a memorable experience, try Egypt via camel.
Above: What's a visit to London without seeing the changing of the guard at Buckingham Palace?

133 Splendor of the Incas
Visit Machu Picchu

This Lost City of the Incas high among the Peruvian Andes is among the most famous archaeological ruins in South America. Built of quarried stone and perched on the mountaintop above the Urubamba River, it's a superb example of the brilliance of the Incan civilization. It's believed that the city was part of a series of fortresses to defend against invaders.

The ruins cover about five square miles and are designed in remarkable harmony with their surroundings. There's even a private lodge overlooking the ruins.

UltimateSplendor:

Hike the Inca Trail, which culminates at Machu Picchu. If hiking is beyond your health or skill level, or doesn't appeal to you, consider seeing Machu Picchu by train.

Reality Check:

If you opt for the trek, it's generally a three- to five-day hike that requires a group and local guide or trek leader.

What It Takes to Get There:

www.gapadventures.com; www.geoex.com; www.iexplore.com; www/blueparallel.com.

Cost: Less than $1,000 for about a week; Machu Picchu by train from Cuzco, about $405 for 4 days; luxury private tour, 5 to 12 days, $4,500 to $6,500.

134 Coast-to-Coast Coasters
Experience the World's Wildest

Flip over, slam sideways, hurl down, and toss about like a rag doll, all at breakneck speed—it's just another day in paradise for roller-coaster junkies.

Junkies come in all ages and sizes. Their passion has no geographic or ethnic boundaries. The chance to experience the fastest, highest, or wildest coaster is the consummation of a dream.

What's your pleasure? Is it hanging over the water or in thin air, in darkness or in light, upside down or right-side up, all of the above or none of the above?

Cringe while blasting from 0 to 128 mph in a few seconds aboard Kingda Ka at Six Flags in New Jersey; thrill at the frightening 80-degree angles of Cedar Point's (Ohio) Millennium Force; lose it at Knott's Berry Farm, California, aboard the Xcelerator; heighten your terror on the inverted Nemesis or vertical drop Oblivion, both at Alton Towers in Staffordshire, England.

Above: Wander the lush ruins at Machu Picchu. Top right: Dare to experience Millennium Force at Cedar Point in Sandusky, Ohio. Bottom right: The sky holds promise over Te Waewae Bay, Southland, New Zealand.

lead. This lack of familiar stars high above can be a bit unsettling or exhilarating for travelers from the Northern Hemisphere. Take your telescope or take a tour. Observatories often feature the opportunity to view the southern sky.

You don't have to head to the Southern Hemisphere, however, to see this heavenly display. The Southern Cross Astronomical Society's annual Winter Star Party in the Florida Keys has designs on the southern heavens, too.

UltimateHeavens:
See the Southern Cross from a sailboat away from the lights of civilization.

Reality Check:
It's an eerie feeling to see a different sky.

What It Takes to Get There:
Southern Cross Astronomical Society, www.scas.org; www.southerntreks.com; www.haciendalosandes.com, click on Other Activities and follow the links; www.discoveryecotours.com.au.

Cost: New Zealand, two-week walking tour and more, about $5,100; one night lodge stay then visit to the observatory Mamalluca in northern Chile, about $195.

UltimateThrill:
Make it a coaster-to-coaster vacation and see the world.

Reality Check:
If you have to ask "Is it safe?" don't try it.

What It Takes to Get There:
www.cedarpoint.com; www.somecoasters.com; www.ultimaterollercoaster.com; www.knotts.com; www.altontowers.com.

Cost: It's not an issue.

Star Light, Star Different
See the Southern Sky

Whether you're a stargazer, adventure seeker, or simply an ordinary traveler in search of the unusual, head way south for a very different angle on the night sky.

Instead of Orion's Belt and the Big Dipper dominating the heavens, the Southern Cross takes the

Legacies, Giving, and Sharing

> *In the final analysis, what we do for and share with others helps us to truly define and understand who we are.*

36 What Empty Nest?
Be There for Your Children

Who says that at 18 years old your child is out of the house and out of your life? Sure, 18 is the age of majority, but in today's complicated, confusing, and very expensive society, many adult children still need their parents' help. Amplifying the need is the incredibly high cost of college, continuing education, and buying a first home.

Providing college tuition or a down payment for a home may be within your means, but be careful that your generosity doesn't go overboard or jeopardize your own financial security.

Another way that many parents help their grown children is by providing full-time or part-time dependable day care for grandchildren. In fact, that's a reason many grown children move closer to home.

Even if a grown child doesn't need financial support, a parent's moral, emotional, and psychological support can make a big difference—just as it did when the child was small.

Reality Check:

If an adult child moves back home, be sure to set household guidelines and include a time line for the move out. That's essential. You might also strongly consider charging nominal rent and a share of the expenses.

What It Takes to Get There:

Intergenerational Programs & Aging, Penn State University, http://intergenerational.cas.psu.edu; Grandparents University, University of Wisconsin Alumni Association, www.uwalumni.com/grandparents.

Cost: Grandparents University, about $140/grandparent, $80/child.

137 Payback Time
Be There for Your Parents

Your parents undoubtedly made many sacrifices on your behalf as they raised you. Now, as your parents age and their needs change, it might be fitting that you make some sacrifices in return. It's payback time.

Sometimes an elderly parent just needs to know you're there to help if the need arises—to run the errands; to provide moral, emotional, or financial support; to handle personal finances; to provide short-term care in an emergency; or simply to offer companionship.

At other times, an ailing or physically weak parent may need your full-time commitment. That means either he or she might move in with you or vice versa. This isn't a decision to be made quickly or taken lightly. It involves much more than the love between a parent and child. Studies have

Left: Sharing time with youngsters the second time around can be most gratifying, especially if those youngsters are your grandchildren. Above: Sometimes an older person just needs to know you're there.

shown that being a full-time caregiver can be draining on your finances as well as on your health and that of your family.

Before you decide to be a full-time caregiver, discuss all the options with your parents, medical caregivers, social workers, and more, and then determine the best approach for your parent's specific situation.

Reality Check:

Being that full-time caregiver truly isn't always the best way to take care of an elderly parent. Adult children sometimes fail to recognize that.

What It Takes to Get There:

http://seniorliving.about.com;
www.thefamilycaregiver.org;
U.S. Administration on Aging, www.aoa.gov,
click on Elders and Families; www.firstgov.gov,
then click on Family, Home and Community;
from the National Hospice and Palliative Care
Organization, www.caringinfo.org.

Cost: From just a few moments of your time to tens of thousands of dollars depending on an elderly parent's needs.

138 Share Your Life
Put Thoughts and Experiences in Writing

Share with your loved ones some of your thoughts, trials and tribulations, feelings, morals, and lessons you have learned while experiencing life by writing an ethical will or even a book of your life. It may not matter that much to you, but it means a great deal to those who come after you.

Think of an ethical will as a letter about your life. It's not a legally binding document like a last will and testament. But it is a legacy to your survivors and future generations. So is your autobiography. Haven't you ever asked yourself, "Why didn't I find out more about that from my mom or dad, uncle, or great-aunt?"

If you're unsure where to begin your own ethical will or life's story, there are books, seminars, and Web sites that can help. Check out the links below.

Reality Check:

What may seem insignificant to you now may go a long way toward helping future generations years from now understand who you were and what it was like growing up through your times.

What It Takes to Get There:

www.ethicalwill.com;
http://yvm.net/vme/ethicalwills;
www.publishingcentral.com, click on Writing;
www.mylifestory.org.

Cost: Writing your thoughts costs nothing but your time. You can, however, opt to spend more money and have the document printed in a way that will preserve it for future generations.

139 Build Your Legacy
Construct a Park or Town Garden in Your Name

For many people, leaving a physical legacy such as a building, park, or garden in the community, country, or world is an important goal in life. It could be payback to the community or humanity in general, or simply a way of sharing one's good fortune and abilities with others.

These physical legacies don't always require a ton of money, either. Donating your time, name, and a limited sum to rally a community to build a playground can leave a lasting impression. So can being a tireless volunteer in a community park or garden. Either could ensure that your moniker is remembered. Drive or walk down the streets in your town and see the various plots of land, buildings, streets, and plazas named after residents who have left their marks.

Of course, donating large amounts of cash, securities, or even your home or another building to a cause helps. In fact, in these post–9/11 days, many nonprofit organizations count more than ever on outside donors to make up potentially massive shortfalls. Even financially strapped public schools look to donations and outside volunteers.

Reality Check:
Before you decide on your building legacy, be sure to check with the potential beneficiary. The group or organization may not really want what you're proposing and may suggest what it considers a better way to spend your money.

What It Takes to Get There:

National Center for Family Philanthropy, www.ncfp.org; National Council of Nonprofit Associations, www.ncna.org; The Philanthropy Roundtable, www.philanthropyroundtable.org.

Cost: Limited only by your generosity.

140 No Time Like the Present
Spend Quality Time with Your Children and Grandchildren

Chances are your grown children want you in their lives if you make the opportunities to be there. Whether you think so or not, you do have a lot to offer them, from love and experience to guidance and companionship.

You can literally share your experiences with your family. Traveling together to your favorite haunts and other significant places is a wonderful way to share your personal history while enjoying one another's company.

Left: Your life story is a gift to future generations. Top: Dr. Lee and Virginia Graver cleared and then donated the land for the arboretum at Muhlenberg College (Bath, Pennsylvania). Above: A Senior Corps volunteer enjoys her work.

If it's been too long since you've seen your children, make that visit happen. If you live out of town and are concerned about being a burden, consider staying at a nearby hotel. You won't insult your child by not staying in his or her home but will help to create a less stressful situation, especially if both of you don't always agree.

This is about having no regrets. If you and a child have had differences in the past, why not consider ironing out those differences and creating a new relationship based on mutual love and understanding. You both still have much to give each other.

Reality Check:
It's not always easy to accept your child as an adult. Conversely, children sometimes have a tough time accepting that their parent is aging.

What It Takes to Get There:
www.familytravelforum.com; www.farhorizon.com; www.aarp.org/families/grandparents.

Cost: Your time.

141 Adopt a Cause
You Can Make a Difference

As an older person, you can make a big difference in your community and beyond by becoming active in a favorite charity or personal cause.

Choose one that appeals to you or work with nonprofit organizations that—free of charge—will help match you with a cause and volunteer opportunities that suit your interests and attitudes. Among those organizations are Senior Corps and AmeriCorps, part of the

Corporation for National & Community Service, and VolunteerMatch.

These groups also are great resources for the volunteer-minded. Check out their Web sites to learn more about how you can help others.

If you can't find a cause that meets your goals and ideals, start your own organization. Either fund it or line up benefactors, and then get out there and start sharing your goodness with others who need it.

Reality Check:
There literally is something for everyone when it comes to volunteering. Spend a vacation volunteering as one way to get started.

What It Takes to Get There:
www.pointsoflight.org; www.volunteermatch.org; Corporation for National & Community Service, www.cns.gov; www.globalvolunteers.com.

Cost: The sky is the limit.

142 Faith in Action
Participate in Your Religion

Congregations, churches, mosques, temples, synagogues, and other religious institutions always need volunteers internally and out in the community.

Among a plethora of opportunities, volunteers may help with after-service coffee and doughnuts or serve as president of an entire congregation;

Above, Top, top right and right: Helping others adds to your enjoyment of your own life. Just ask these volunteers with the Corporation for National & Community Service.

act as a deacon or lay spiritual leader; teach religious education classes for young and old; work as volunteer secretary or treasurer; spread their faith locally and worldwide; or participate in outreach to the poor, incarcerated, sick, elderly, and others needing help.

Whatever your skills, no matter how menial you might consider them, volunteer. Even if you simply open mail or run errands, you're providing a valuable service to a nonprofit organization that depends on the generosity of your time and energy.

If you don't belong to a religious group, consider volunteering with a local or regional nondenominational council. Such groups often coordinate efforts to create a better community for all.

Reality Check:
Be careful of scams. Always check an organization's track record and references before volunteering with them.

What It Takes to Get There:

Check with individual religious organizations in your area; www.networkforgood.org; www.idealist.org; www.pointsoflight.org/networks/faith.

Cost: Your time.

Into the Future
Establish a Trust to Help Others

Whether you think big or small, a trust is your opportunity to go on helping others after you die. It's a living legacy. By establishing and funding a trust, you dictate what is to be done with the money in that trust and when.

It could be an ideal way to hold property or assets for the benefit of a person, persons, or organization. You can set up a trust to pay for a grandchild's future college education, for example, or even to solidify the future finances of a favorite cause. If you support an organization and are concerned about what will happen to it after you're gone, you can set up a trust designating the cause as your beneficiary, thus ensuring its future.

A trust doesn't require a fortune, either. If you're a lifelong music teacher, a few thousand dollars in a trust could establish a music scholarship in your community.

Reality Check:
If you're considering donating sizable assets to a trust with beneficiaries other than family members, be sure to talk it over with your family first. It's your money and your decision, but your family, at the very least, should be aware of your wishes beforehand. Also beware of preprinted forms. It's best to have a qualified attorney put together your documents.

What It Takes to Get There:

Check with a qualified legal and financial advisor; www.pueblo.gsa.gov, then type "trust" into the search engine; American Bar Association, www.abanet.org; www.martindale.com.

Cost: Varies dramatically depending on the type of trust, its complexity, and more.

144 Spread Goodness Worldwide
Join or Work with Organizations

Travel the world and build peace, understanding, and friendship at the same time. This can be your rewarding reality as a volunteer with a variety of organizations worldwide.

U.S. Servas, for example, is an international host and traveler network that promotes peace and understanding in more than 135 countries.

Groups like the Peace Corps, United Nations Volunteers for Peace and Development, Global Volunteers, World Volunteer Web, and the International Association for Volunteer Effort spearhead or act as clearinghouses for humanitarian volunteer projects.

Reality Check:

Certain physical risks may be associated with some geographic areas in which volunteers are needed.

What It Takes to Get There:

www.usservas.org; United Nations Volunteers for Peace and Development, www.unv.org; Global Volunteers, www.globalvolunteers.com; World Volunteer Web, www.worldvolunteerweb.org; International Association for Volunteer Effort, www.iave.org; www.idealist.org.

Cost: Your time and often travel costs. Some organizations offer stipends and reimburse for expenses.

145 Retirees Helping Seniors
Help the Elderly Stay in Their Homes

Use your own good health and good fortune to help less fortunate peers maintain their independent lives and dignity.

The elderly—even those who are financially secure—often depend on outside help from volunteers like you so they can stay in their own homes. The alternative can be assisted living or a nursing home.

These seniors might need help running errands or a ride to the grocery store, a hot meal delivered regularly to their door, transportation to and from medical care, yard work, winterizing or summerizing their home, or just a friendly face to let them know someone still cares.

You can be that someone. The gratitude of those you help can be overwhelming. Even the smallest kindness makes a difference to these Americans who often feel as if the world has passed them by.

Above and right: Global Volunteers Dennis Killeen, above in the Cook Islands, and Anne Scanlon, right at Camp Hope in Quito, Ecuador, spread special goodness. Top right: A smile brightens a day.

Consider volunteering with a local Meals on Wheels or government or religious group that assists seniors. Many local, state, and national organizations are eager for your help.

Reality Check:

It can be gut-wrenching to see how families have simply forgotten or cast aside the elderly.

What It Takes to Get There:

Contact local senior organizations; Corporation for National & Community Service, www.nationalservice.gov; Senior Corps, www.seniorcorps.gov; www.aoa.gov, click on Elders and Families; Meals on Wheels, www.mowaa.org.

Cost: Generally only your time.

The Hope of the Future
Help the Children of the World

Just as the elderly often are forgotten, so are the children of the world. They frequently are the true victims of war and conflict in the streets at home and the roads abroad. As a result, their legacy becomes one of poverty, pain, and suffering.

Often by helping just a little you can make a tremendous difference in these children's lives; if you're willing to do much more, yours is a true legacy.

Consider working with any of the many groups worldwide to help orphans and disadvantaged children—including those in the United States. You might mentor through a Big Brothers, Big Sisters program in your town, volunteer in an orphanage across the globe, or donate money and goods to victims of wars, disasters, and famines.

Reality Check:

Don't always judge other countries by Western standards. In some cases, the way a country treats its orphans is the best possible under the circumstances. Other times, children are exploited and abused for profit and personal gain.

What It Takes to Get There:

National Association of Foster Grandparents, www.nafgpd.org; www.bigbrothersbigsisters.org; www.childadvocates.org; www.globalvolunteers.org; www.globalcrossroad.com.

Cost: However much you can afford to donate or simply your time.

Helping others in their hour of need is a most worthy way to volunteer your time. But a word of caution: Being the first (or second) responder on the scene of disaster can be emotionally as well as physically taxing. On a brighter note, it also can be one of the most rewarding forms of volunteerism.

Perhaps the most recognizable organization in any disaster, large or small, is the Red Cross. Its Web site has an easy-to-use volunteer match system. Religious groups, nondenominational and otherwise, also are early-on-the-scene providers.

Reality Check:
Not all disaster volunteers need to be on the scene. Those in behind-the-scenes support roles are vital, too. Even the amateur-radio community plays an important role in providing help in disasters.

What It Takes to Get There:

www.redcross.org, then click on Volunteer; www.volunteersolutions.org; Corporation for National & Community Service, www.nationalservice.gov; Senior Corps, www.seniorcorps.gov.

Cost: Your time.

147 Mitigating Disaster
Volunteer to Help the Victims

When Hurricane Katrina slammed Louisiana and Mississippi and left devastation and disaster for hundreds of thousands of people in its wake, when the terrifying tsunami hit Southeast Asia in 2004 and washed away tens of thousands of lives and livelihoods, when back-to-back hurricanes brought massive destruction to Florida that same year, or even when a fire destroys a home and displaces a family down the street, organizations and volunteers are there to help. Some provide physical relief—food, shelter, and clothing. Others offer a soothing word or comforting presence.

Save the Earth
Help Preserve Our Environment

Your financial donations can and do make a difference to the Earth.

Organizations like the Nature Conservancy and the Conservation Fund work with communities and other organizations to purchase what they perceive as threatened habitats or lands with the goal of protecting and preserving them. Literally millions of acres of land and thousands of miles of rivers, streams, shoreline, and other habitats worldwide have been preserved, thanks to the efforts of these and other conservation organizations.

Much of the funding comes from environmentally conscious citizens who want to make a difference. If you're one of those people, check out some of the organizations' Web sites. They often detail options for giving.

If you have a better idea on conservation, do your part and then spread the conservation word yourself. Start your own conservation group.

Reality Check:
The Earth and its environment is an apolitical issue. It's everyone's concern.

What It Takes to Get There:

www.thenatureconservancy.org;
www.conservationfund.org;
www.deltalandtrust.org;
www.earthrestorationservice.org.

Cost: Depends on the degree of your generosity.

The Gift of Peace
Volunteer for Hospice

Hospice brings serenity and comfort to the dying process both for the living and the terminally ill. Virtually anyone who has ever sought out hospice to help a dying friend or loved one understands the gift of its dignity and peace.

That gift depends a great deal on tens of thousands of volunteers like you who are willing to donate their time and more.

Perhaps volunteering means holding the hand of a dying mother and a grieving child, or vice versa, in a hospice facility. Or it could mean running errands or providing respite care or companionship for in-home hospice.

Top left: After the 1989 earthquake in San Francisco, volunteers helped the city pick up. Left: Global Volunteer David Denton works in the rain forests of Kauai. Above: A volunteer makes a difference to the living and the dying.

Perhaps this is your opportunity to make a difference in the end-of-life situation of your peers. If you're not sure whether volunteering with hospice is right for you, you might see if you can tag along with a volunteer to witness the difference it makes.

Reality Check:

As a hospice volunteer, you help not only the dying but the living, too.

What It Takes to Get There:

Check with local hospices or www.hospicefoundation.org; http://www.hospices.org; www.aoa.gov, then click on Elders and Families.

Cost: Your time.

150 # A Friend to Animals
Support Organizations and Shelters

Every year thousands of unwanted or abused pets and animals rely on human beings for help. Animal shelters and sanctuaries, including Noah's Wish, need money, support, and, often, volunteers. Other international nonprofit groups like the World Wildlife Fund work to protect endangered species and their habitats, and welcome donations and activism.

A horse rescue desperately needs extra hay to feed an influx of abused and starving animals. A pet sanctuary needs more space or money to expand its overflowing facilities. No-longer-wanted exotic animals or retired circus animals

may need a place to live their remaining years in relative comfort rather than be killed. Natural disasters, too, prompt special needs for animals. Wildfires, for example, often lead to forced evacuations of livestock that requires shelter and feed. Thousands of pets also were left stranded and homeless by Hurricane Katrina.

Donate money; volunteer your time; care for an unwanted or sick animal; give equipment and more to local shelters; be a foster parent for a young animal; or think about getting involved in the World Wildlife Fund's Conservation Action Network.

Reality Check:
Check with local, national, and international organizations to find out how you can help.

What It Takes to Get There:

World Wildlife Fund, www.wwfus.org; Best Friends Animal Society, www.bestfriends.org; The Humane Society of the United States, www.hsus.org; www.bigcatrescue.org; www.noahswish.org.

Cost: As little as your time.

Volunteer Vacations
Your Time Is Invaluable

Next time you're thinking about taking a typical, self-indulgent vacation for a few days, weeks, or months, think instead about combining great travel opportunities with helping others. Take a volunteer vacation.

Teach English to children in Sri Lanka. Care for big cats in South Africa. Help with reforestation in Ecuador. Work with prehistoric pottery in Arizona. Clean up an old battleship in Hawaii. Help the kids

at a rural orphanage in the Ukraine. These are a few of the many different vacations that offer travelers more than just a getaway to recharge the body. Volunteer vacations reinvigorate the mind, body, and soul of travelers of all ages.

Make friends in different worlds and leave behind a legacy of goodness, kindness, and camaraderie.

Reality Check:
Volunteer vacations aren't for everyone. Consider your health, what comfort level you're willing to accept, and the safety and politics of a potential volunteer destination before making any decision on whether to do it.

What It Takes to Get There:

www.globalvolunteers.org; www.responsibletravel.com; www.unitedplanet.org, then click on Volunteer; www.elderhostel.org, then click on Programs; www.i-to-i.com.

Cost: Peru service program about $2,000 through Global Volunteers; coach baseball in the Dominican Republic, $1,395 and up (www.i-to-i.com).

Left: An animal finds solace after a disaster thanks to the nonprofit Noah's Wish. Above: Through Global Volunteers, Eliana Garcia spends her vacation teaching children in Lima, Peru.

Resources

Here are just a few of the many Web sites that can provide valuable information on your quest to find your retirement. Be sure to check out the many books, magazines, pamphlets, and more available from organizations and libraries, too.

Government

U.S. Administration on Aging: Excellent source of information on all kinds of topics, www.aoa.gov

FirstGov: U.S. government Web portal to government agencies and more, www.firstgov.gov

Housing

HSH Associates: Source on the finances of home ownership, www.hsh.com

National Association of Realtors: Information, links, and more to topics related to housing and property ownership, www.realtor.org

Information

AARP: Information, advocacy, travel, and benefits for people ages 50 and up, www.aarp.org

About.com: Information, travel, shopping, and more, www.about.com

Google: Search engine, www.google.com

Hillman Wonders of the World: Information and photos of "The World's Top 100 Wonders," www.hillmanwonders.com

Museum of Unnatural Mystery: Information on unusual places, including the Wonders of the World, www.unmuseum.org

Nations Online Project: A portal of gateways to information and more on countries, cultures, and nations, www.nationsonline.org

Suddenly Senior: Senior trivia, travel, links, and more, www.suddenlysenior.com

U.S. Administration on Aging: Excellent source of information on all kinds of topics, www.aoa.gov

Yahoo!: Portal to all kinds of information, including travel, www.yahoo.com

Legal

ALM Law: Legal news and information, including lawyer locator, www.law.com

American Bar Association: Legal news and information, including lawyer locator, www.abanet.org

LexisNexis® Martindale-Hubbell®: Legal information, resources, lawyer locator, www.martindale.com

Nolo: Self-help legal information, books source, www.nolo.com

Politics

Gray Panthers: Information and advocacy, www.graypanthers.org

League of Women Voters: Nonpartisan political organization, www.lwv.org

Travel

AARP: Information, advocacy, travel, and benefits for people ages 50 and up, www.aarp.org

A1 Vacation Properties: Private condos, apartments, villas, and other housing options, www.a1vacationproperties.com

About.com: Information, travel, shopping, and more, www.about.com

Away.com: Travel guides and advice, http://away.com

BootsnAllTravel: Resource for independent travelers, www.bootsnall.com

Cruise Web: All about cruises, cruising, hot links, discounts, and more, www.cruiseweb.com

Xe.com: Currency converter, www.xe.com

CyberRentals: Private condos, apartments, villas, and other housing options, www.cyberrentals.com

Earthwatch Institute: Conservation, research, volunteering, expeditions, www.earthwatch.org

Elderhostel: Education and travel for older adults, www.elderhostel.org

50plus Expeditions: Adventure travel for people over age 50, www.50plusexpeditions.com

Fodor's Online Travel Guides: Guidebooks, information, reservations, and more, www.fodors.com

G.A.P Adventures: Adventures and tours, www.gapadventures.com

Geographic Expeditions: Adventure trips, treks, voyages, and tours, www.geoex.com

Globus®: Tours, travel packages, and more worldwide, www.globusjourneys.com

GoNomad™: Alternative travel, ecotourism, and destination guides, www.gonomad.com

Great Hawaii Vacations: Hawaii hotels, resorts, condo rentals, and more, www.greathawaiivacations.com

Great Rentals: Private condos, apartments, villas, and other housing options, www.greatrentals.com

The Grueninger Group: Tour specialists, including music, rail, and cruises, www.grueningertours.com

HomeLink International: Worldwide home and house vacation exchange, www.homelink.org.uk

KOA Kampgrounds of America: All things related to camping and RVing, including camp, cabin, lodge directory, www.koa.com

Lonely Planet: Guidebooks, travel advice, information, www.lonelyplanet.com

Marybeth Bond—The Gutsy Traveler: Travel, tips, resources, and more, www.gutsytraveler.com

National Park Service: Everything about U.S. national parks, including hot links to individual park Web sites, www.nps.gov

Pilot Guides.com: Online travel magazine, destination guide, www.pilotguides.com

Rail Europe Group: Source for rail-related travel, including rail passes, in Europe and lots more, www.raileurope.com

Real Adventures: Travel, adventure, accommodations, and more, www.realadventures.com

Travel with a Challenge Magazine: Senior travel, culture, cruises, nature vacations, www.travelwithachallenge.com

Trip Advisor.com: Hotels, resorts, travel packages, great reviews, www.tripadvisor.com.

VacationHomes.com: Private condos, apartments, villas, and other housing options, www.vacationhomes.com

Vacation Rentals.com: Private condos, apartments, villas, and other housing options, www.vacationrentals.com

Where in the World Travel: Travel adventures and events, with links, www.whereintheworld.co.uk

Volunteering/Philanthropy

American Red Cross: Disaster and aid-relief experts, www.redcross.org

AmeriCorps: A program of the Corporation for National & Community Service, network or local, state, and national service programs, www.americorps.org

Corporation for National & Community Service: Organization to help Americans provide services to meet community needs, www.nationalservice.gov

Global Volunteers: International volunteers working for peace through service, www.globalvolunteer.org

National Council of Nonprofit Associations: Network of state and regional associations of nonprofits, www.ncna.org

Network for Good: Connects individuals with their favorite charitable causes, www.networkforgood.org

Points of Light Foundation and Volunteer Center National Network: Engages and mobilizes volunteers to solve social problems in communities, www.pointsoflight.org

United Planet: Volunteer, learn, share cultures, peace, www.unitedplanet.org

World Volunteer Web: Global one-stop-shop for information, resources, and organizations linked to volunteerism, www.worldvolunteerweb.org

Senior Corps: Connects those over 55 with people and organizations in need, including RSVP; a program of the Corporation for National & Community Service, www.seniorcorps.org

VolunteerMatch: Internet recruiting tool that matches volunteers and organizations in need, www.volunteermatch.org

Credits

Photography and illustration credits are listed by page in the order which they are read.

76 Photo courtesy of NASA

77 Robert Llewellyn/SuperStock;
Photo courtesy of Rainbow Trout Ranch,
Colorado/Dude Ranchers' Association

78 William Strode/SuperStock

79 Photo courtesy of Ilene Perlman

80 Gala/SuperStock

81 Ferrell McCollough/SuperStock;
Angelo Cavalli/SuperStock

82 age fotostock/SuperStock

83 Hugh Burden/SuperStock

84 Photo courtesy of Bart Barlow/Tishman Speyer

85 Kwame Zikomo/SuperStock

86 Adamsmith/SuperStock

87 age fotostock/SuperStock

88 Dale Wilson/Masterfile

89 age fotostock/SuperStock;
Photo courtesy of Castle Stuart/Inverness

90 Photo courtesy of Vassi Koutsaftis/
www.geoex.com

91 Brian Lawrence/SuperStock

92 age fotostock/SuperStock

93 age fotostock/SuperStock

94 age fotostock/SuperStock

95 Kathleen Finlay/Masterfile

96 Photo courtesy of Holger Leue

97 Sherman Hines/Masterfile

98 SuperStock, Inc./SuperStock;
Photo courtesy of Blue Lagoon—
Geothermal Spa, Iceland

99 Bryan Reinhart/Masterfile;
Steve Vidler/SuperStock

100 Bryan Reinhart/Masterfile

101 Steve Vidler/SuperStock

102 age fotostock/SuperStock;
Bob Gelberg/Masterfile

103 John Warden/SuperStock

104 Photo courtesy of Thomas Loof

105 age fotostock/SuperStock;
Tom Murphy/SuperStock

106 Photo courtesy of Priscilla R. Summers

107 Photo courtesy of Douglas Peebles/
www.douglaspeebles.com

108 Richard Cummins/SuperStock

109 Miles Ertman/Masterfile; Photo courtesy of
Douglas Peebles/www.douglaspeebles.com

110 Daryl Benson/Masterfile

111 Stief & Schnare/SuperStock;
Dean Fox/SuperStock

112 SuperStock, Inc./SuperStock

113 Daryl Benson/Masterfile

114 Kurt Scholz/SuperStock

115 Daryl Benson/Masterfile;
Ron Dahlquist/SuperStock

116 Horst Klemm/Masterfile

117 George Contorakes/Masterfile

118 Gail Mooney/Masterfile

119 Peter Christopher/Masterfile;
David Zimmerman/Masterfile

120 age fotostock/SuperStock

121 Bryan Reinhart/Masterfile

122 Lloyd Sutton/Masterfile

123 age fotostock/SuperStock;
John de Visser/Masterfile

124 Ron Dahlquist/SuperStock

125 Larry Fisher/Masterfile;
Peter Christopher/Masterfile

126 Photo courtesy of G.A.P Adventures

127 Photo courtesy of Cedar Point
Amusement Park/Resort, Sandusky, Ohio;
SuperStock, Inc./SuperStock

128 Kevin Dodge/Masterfile

129 Kevin Dodge/Masterfile

130 age fotostock/SuperStock

131 Michael P. Gadomski/SuperStock;
Photo courtesy of Corporation for
National & Community Service

132 Photo courtesy of Corporation for
National & Community Service

133 Photos courtesy of Corporation for
National & Community Service

134 Photo courtesy of Global Volunteers

135 Jiang Jin/SuperStock;
Photo courtesy of Global Volunteers

136 Roy King/SuperStock;
    Photo courtesy of Global Volunteers

137 Powerstock/SuperStock

138 Photo courtesy of Noah's Wish

139 Photo courtesy of Global Volunteers

Back Cover Brian MacDonald, MacDonald Photography

Book design by Pletka Design, Naperville, IL